Praise for *Tarot Spreads*

"Meg Jones Wall lays out the art of tarot spreads with clarity, heart, and precision. *Tarot Spreads: How to Read Them, Create Them & Revise Them* offers readers the tools to move beyond one-card pulls and into intentional, customized layouts that bring structure, nuance, and insight to any reading. Rooted in lived experience and crafted with care, this book is an essential resource for tarot readers looking to deepen their practice and design spreads that truly speak. It's authentic, accessible, and a testament to Meg's gift for teaching through her writing."

—Mat Auryn, author of *The Psychic Art of Tarot* and *Psychic Witch*

"Author Meg Jones Wall has written the ultimate book for tarot spread enthusiasts! *Tarot Spreads: How to Read Them, Create Them & Revise Them* is the most comprehensive book I've ever read on this topic. Every aspect for creating personalized tarot spreads is here, from why you might want to design your own layouts to how to test and fine-tune your creations. Practical advice, thoughtful prompts, and a library of 'spreads for every occasion' make this book useful for all tarot readers. Keep this one close by—it might quickly become the most used book in your tarot library."

—Theresa Reed, author of *The Cards You're Dealt* and *Tarot: No Quesions Asked*

"Meg Jones Wall's *Tarot Spreads* offers something crucial and unexpected beyond beginner books and the innumerable spreads that proliferate the internet: a balance of freedom and stability. While 'how to read tarot' books may tell you what the cards mean and spreads inform which questions to ask, Wall leaves those largely open to your discretion and instead digs into how and why tarot works. For many of us, especially neurodivergent folks, we need more specific operationalized guidance between 'ask a question,' 'draw cards,' and 'interpret the meaning' to feel secure that we know what we're doing. This book offers exactly that, going into particular depth about what makes a good question and how, when, and why (or why not) to use a spread for a reading. For certain this is a great new intro to tarot; I think many seasoned readers will find that some unexplored or overly rigid aspects of their early learning are addressed helpfully in this book as well."

—Lane Smith, author of
78 Acts of Liberation: Tarot to Transform Our World

"A perfect book to be in conversation with your other tarot texts, regardless of whether you're looking for information on spreads specifically or just looking to go next level in your tarot practice. Wall's work perfectly breaks down why things work the way they do while giving you plenty of space to dream and experiment."

—Cassandra Snow, author of *Tarot in Other Words*
and *Queering the Tarot*

TAROT SPREADS

Also by Meg Jones Wall

Finding the Fool: A Tarot Journey to Radical Transformation

TAROT SPREADS

How to Read Them, Create Them & Revise Them

MEG JONES WALL

WEISER BOOKS

This edition first published in 2025 by Weiser Books, an imprint of
Red Wheel/Weiser, LLC
With offices at:
65 Parker Street, Suite 7
Newburyport, MA 01950
www.redwheelweiser.com

ISBN: 978-1-57863-855-0
Library of Congress Cataloging-in-Publication Data
Names: Wall, Meg Jones, 1985- author.
Title: Tarot spreads : how to read them, create them, and revise them / Meg Jones Wall.
Description: Newburyport, MA : Weiser Books, 2025. | Summary: "From single-card readings to twenty-card layouts, tarot spreads help to bring structure, clarity, and purpose to tarot readings. But for many readers, spreads can feel confusing, hard to read, or just plain frustrating. If a reading seems off or just doesn't resonate, you don't need to use the tarot spread as it's written, and you don't need to start from scratch. This book will help tarot readers of all skill and experience levels to develop their own personalized spreads or tweak existing spreads to better suit their needs"-- Provided by publisher.
Identifiers: LCCN 2025003578 | ISBN 9781578638550 (trade paperback) | ISBN 9781633413535 (ebook) Subjects: LCSH: Tarot. | Tarot cards. Classification: LCC BF1879.T2 W3333 2025 | DDC 133.3/2424--dc23/eng/20250321
LC record available at https://lccn.loc.gov/2025003578

Cover design by Sky Peck Design
Interior by Steve Amarillo / Urban Design, LLC
Typeset in Adobe Arno Pro and Bebas Neue

Printed in the United States of America
IBI
10 9 8 7 6 5 4 3 2 1

CONTENTS

INTRODUCTION

You should know that my first attempts to read and write tarot spreads, like my first attempts to learn how to read tarot, went horribly.

I didn't really know what a spread might have to offer my tarot practice, if I'm being honest. I didn't know how to use spreads or even how they worked. I just felt that the general readings that I'd been doing were starting to feel a little lacking and knew that I wanted more detail, more information, more insights. Just *more*.

The world was scary and hard, and I needed support. My mental health was in a particularly low place, it was Trump's first term, everyone I knew was in a complete panic, and my startup job was systematically eliminating everyone who had been hired at the same time that I was—never a good sign in the wake of a major tech acquisition. I wanted more specificity than my daily single-card readings were giving me, and I thought that a spread might help me see the situations that I was struggling with through a clearer lens. To my mind, additional cards might somehow crack my world wide open.

They did—but not in the way that I'd expected. With no idea what I was doing, I decided to try out the classic ten-card Celtic Cross, a spread that seems ubiquitous within the tarot world, shared in every tarot resource I found—a layout that so many revered and respected. The positions as written didn't really make sense to me, but I decided to go for it anyway. I figured that if everyone was using it, this must be a spread that was relatively accessible. I hoped that after I'd pulled cards, I would magically understand how the prompts worked together and would see what so many others seemed to see when they used this well-known spread.

What a choice I made! That ambitious reading left me scratching my head, frustrated and confused, wondering just what the hell I'd thought I was doing. There were so many different things happening in the reading, and I didn't understand the positions, the flow, the *point* of any of it. It was just me and a pile of cards, adrift in a sea of meanings and contradictions. I spent hours trying to decipher that reading but eventually gave up, putting the deck away and feeling less certain about my ability to do complex tarot readings than ever.

In the wake of that attempt, I felt as though I'd jumped straight into the deep end when I couldn't even tread water. I'd finally gotten a handle on reading tarot in general, but after that experience, I wondered if spreads simply weren't for me, or if I wasn't the kind of reader who should be trying to use them. Maybe I just needed to stick to my simple single-card readings and leave the spreads to the pros. Maybe I still had way more to learn about the tarot itself before I could read multiple cards together without getting completely lost.

Eventually, as so often happens, my curiosity got the better of me, and I wanted to try again. This time, I left the long and complex spreads behind and chose a simple three-card layout with positions that I actually understood. It was a new moon spread, concise and straightforward, and I was eager to see how reading with it might go. This time, my reading was just as short, sweet, and clear as the spread itself. I understood both what I was asking *and* how the cards were answering my questions. And I could see how the spread had helped to provide much-needed guardrails around my inquiries, guiding the conversation in a direction that felt supportive, encouraging, and even kind.

After that, I was hooked. I used spreads in my tarot readings all the time. I spent hours online, looking for new spreads to try out.

Sometimes I didn't understand why the prompts seemed repetitive, while other times I felt as though the spread was a bit abrupt. Regardless of how clear the readings themselves were, I loved exploring people's ideas and was in awe of the tarot experts who had put them together.

Those spreads felt like magic. They still do. At the time I wondered how spread writers found their inspiration, how they knew what the positions should be, how they learned to make such a special tool. The writing of spreads felt like a sacred act somehow. Because I was a tarot newbie, still fumbling through my readings and constantly researching cards to find meanings that made sense for my questions, it never occurred to me that I might one day be well known for my own original tarot spreads. I simply hoped that one day I would know the secrets of writing a great spread, that I might eventually be experienced enough to be able to create layouts like the ones I loved.

I wish I had a better story for you. But the honest truth is that the first time I wrote my own tarot spread, I repeated my initial mistakes and made things much harder for myself than necessary. I was emotional and lonely and was desperate for advice from the cards. In other words, I was not really in a place to do an intensive tarot reading—but went for it anyway. After scouring the internet for several days and not finding a spread that really seemed appropriate for my unique heartbreak, I figured that I could just whip up my own and started copying down individual positions from spreads I'd seen in my research. No position that I liked got rejected. If it felt relevant to my feelings and the matter at hand, I added it to the spread. It was in this emotional state that I decided that using this rambling and untested spread for myself, on this deeply tender topic, with no additional support or objectivity, was a great idea.

Reader, it was not. This spread was a kitchen sink of prompts, with no flow, no end point, and a bevy of positions that asked the same questions over and over. Even with so many cards crammed into the layout, I hadn't added any supportive or encouraging positions for myself—only prompts for finding clarity and recognizing emotion, cards that I thought would acknowledge me and my complicated feelings. As I shuffled and drew cards for the reading, every new card about frustration and anger and loneliness left me feeling worse and worse about myself. By the time I had the full reading laid out in front of me and was looking at fourteen cards of grief, pain, and leaving things behind, I burst into tears. The reading may have been technically "right" in that it accurately represented how I was feeling, but it certainly didn't help me feel any *better* or show me what I could do to repair my situation in any meaningful way. I'd made myself into a punching bag, and had turned an already tender situation into something even worse by thoughtlessly using a bloated tarot spread that didn't address my actual needs.

That first experience of writing a tarot spread left me shaken, and I swore up and down that I wouldn't try again. I'd flown too close to the sun, so to speak, and I told myself that I had used a technique that was far too advanced for my skill set. Yet there was a little piece of me that still wanted to try, that still stubbornly believed that I might be able to one day write a spread that was balanced and clear, supportive and inspiring. In spite of how difficult my relationship with tarot spreads had been over the years, there was a little voice in my head that said that with so many people out there creating layouts, writing spreads couldn't *possibly* require psychic skills or deep magic or decades of experience: it just required more practice.

By now, you've probably noticed a pattern in my general approach to tarot (and, if I'm being honest, to life): I try something new, it doesn't work out as planned, and I wonder if I should just give up . . . before eventually trying again anyway. Perhaps it's my stubbornly obsessive sixth house Scorpio sun or my endlessly curious chart ruler of Mercury in Sagittarius, but I often loop back around to the things I want to learn, determined to get it right even if I've messed up a hundred times in the past. And that's exactly how writing tarot spreads went: eventually, I wanted to try again.

And eventually, I figured out how to write spreads that actually worked—not just in general, but spreads that I also liked using, that provided clarity and comfort in equal measure, that made sense to me and to other people. I prioritized writing shorter spreads, since that's what I actually liked to use. I wrote prompts that felt clear to me and figured out what kinds of positions I liked in my spreads to leave me feeling supported instead of clobbered by my cards, even if the messages I received were difficult to sit with. I also abandoned predictive final cards, opting instead for advice or encouragement or insights, building in the freedom to choose that I craved instead of leaving me worried that I was already locked into a specific fate.

Getting to this point has been a long series of trials and errors and practice, blended with some actual magic. But now, spreads often pop into my head fully formed, like generous gifts offered straight from the clever hands of Mercury. Now, I can quickly write a tarot spread that flows like water and sparks like flames, that grounds in earth or soars through the air, that gets deeply into the heart of a matter or playfully skims across the surface. Now, I write spreads for social media and for my newsletter and for clients, bespoke spreads and quick-and-dirty spreads, powerful spreads and ridiculous spreads. And in putting together spread collections for this book, I found myself not only scrolling back through hundreds and hundreds of spreads I've written but also whipping up new ones with ease.

I don't say all of this to brag. I say this because I can teach you to do it too. This book will walk you through reading spreads as well as writing and revising original spreads, giving you everything you need to understand, develop, tweak, and test tarot spreads of your very own. Whether you come to this book loving tarot spreads and hungry for more, or whether you've had a bad experience reading spreads and are skeptical of ever enthusiastically using them again, I've got something for you here.

• • •

Tarot spreads can be intimidating.

If you're new to the practice of working with prewritten card layouts, then an image with a dozen or more cards laid out in a precise shape, with each card corresponding to a series of elaborate questions, might feel overwhelming, confusing, or inaccessible. It may seem that a spread has a lot of rules and expectations, with a low threshold for error.

But please, release yourself from the expectation that you need to use a spread precisely as written in order to get the full benefit of this layout in your reading. Spreads are infinitely customizable and can be adjusted to suit your own needs, preferences, and experience level.

For example, there is a brilliant tarot spread in the world called the "Horseshoe Spread," which is typically presented as a seven-card spread arranged in a U shape. Sometimes the U opens upwards like the letter—other times it's upside-down, opening downwards. The cards are often numbered, as in the example below, offering a guide to the order for drawing and interpreting the cards. Sometimes you'll also see a key written below the image, explaining what each card's prompt is—but other times, the prompt will be written inside of the card's outline, making for a more concise image.

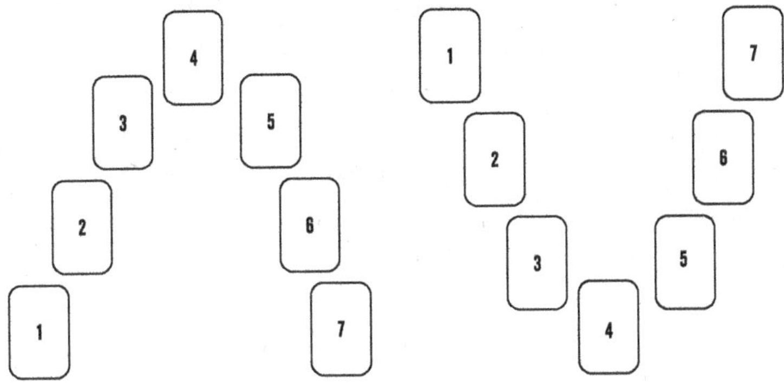

These details make for an impressive-looking spread. But what I want you to remember, whether you're pulling seven cards or twelve cards or twenty cards, is that the shape that the cards make doesn't really matter at all. Tarot spreads aren't about elaborate layouts or following a diagram precisely—spreads are instead about using the cards to create and interpret a meaningful, personal story. This Horseshoe Spread would work just as well if you laid the cards out in a single line of seven cards, or two lines, or a circle, or anything else you like. What the image offers you is a map of how many cards you're pulling in total and a reminder to pull cards one at a time. If you choose to pull cards in a different order or arrange them in a different shape, that's entirely up to you. You are the reader who guides the reading, sets the pace, and finds the flow—the spread is simply the starting point.

Because of how intimidating tarot spreads can be, there's an argument to be made that simply using tarot spreads at all is an intermediate tarot technique. But I firmly believe that readers at any level can use spreads if they are willing to put in the appropriate time, energy, and patience. For some, using spreads may feel natural and intuitive; for others, this could be a challenging thing to incorporate into your practice. But you can benefit from my mistakes and not have to repeat them. I'll walk you through everything you need to know.

By the time you reach the big tarot spread collection in Part Five of this book, you'll know exactly how to use those spreads in your own practice—and will even be empowered to edit or adjust them for your own needs.

PART ONE

BEFORE WE BEGIN

If you've picked up this book, I'm assuming that you are relatively familiar with tarot cards, the process of reading tarot, and what a tarot spread is. In the spirit of being thorough, the following is a very brief introduction to tarot itself, its history, and its uses.

What *Is* Tarot?

Tarot is, at a base level, a deck of cards. They're usually slightly longer and wider than a standard fifty-two-card poker-style playing card deck, but they always have at least seventy-eight cards in them and follow the same structure regardless of art style and imagery.

Common assumptions are that tarot cards are used primarily for fortune-telling or are used exclusively by psychics, but in truth tarot cards can be used for basically anything: from divination and personal spirituality work to community care, creative practices, communication with ancestors or deities, advice, conversation starters, or anything else you can think of. Tarot was not just one thing to one group of people. It contains multitudes.

In terms of structure, all tarot decks have seventy-eight cards. (Other occult decks exist, including Lenormand cards, Kippur cards, oracle cards, and angel cards, but these are distinct from tarot decks and follow their own rules.) Some modern decks will add extra archetypes to the major arcana, and different decks may follow different traditions, which lead to different naming conventions. But a tarot deck is always structured the same way, into two sections.

The first section is made up of twenty-two major arcana cards, also known as archetypes or trumps, that speak to major life moments, transformative experiences, important choices, or necessary revelations. This is often referred to as the Fool's Journey and features figures, energies, and forces that we can experience, harness, work with, or acknowledge. These are the cards that are most often featured in media, that are held up as particularly scary or lovely or impactful—the cards that are the most likely to be recognized by someone who has no familiarity with tarot.

While my previous book, *Finding the Fool*, goes into much more depth with the keywords, correspondences, and potential interpretations of these cards, I'm including here some general meanings for each card as a jumping-off point. Tarot is incredibly personal, and you may have completely different perspectives on these archetypes than the ones presented here—and that is absolutely fine and wonderful. Consider the following to be quick introductions to each card, rather than an exhaustive understanding of all that these archetypes contain. To help you integrate your own unique understandings of these cards, this book uses extremely simple, non-deck-specific illustrations that focus on key elements of each archetype, inspired by the well-known symbolism within the Rider-Waite-Smith deck. Feel free to use whatever tarot deck resonates for you, and to build on these descriptions within your own practice.

The Archetypes

FOOL: desire, trust in the self, fresh start, new journey, leap of faith, freedom, aspiration, radical thinking, rebellion and revolution, hope, change

MAGICIAN: sparks of insight and inspiration, high energy, potential, anticipation, courage, vision, confidence, brainstorming, imagination, trailblazing

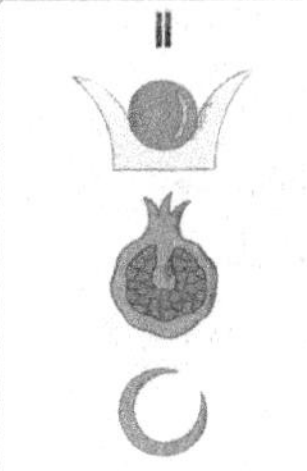

PRIESTESS: observation, crossroads, patience, inner wisdom, self-trust, deliberation, balance, mystery, intuition, receptivity, awareness

EMPRESS: abundance, creativity, generosity, values, collaboration, expression, manifestation, growth, community, care, expansion, joy, pleasure, being present

EMPEROR: discipline, organization, control, long-term planning, foundations, structure, systems, leadership, authority, worthiness, traditions, ambition, caution

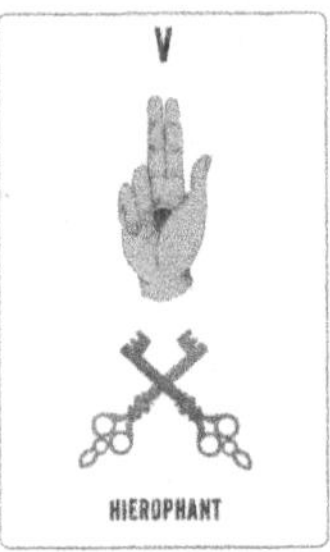

HIEROPHANT: education, knowledge, wisdom, gathering information, exploration, examination, ritual, history, testing limits, intellectual and spiritual adventure, humility, movement, change

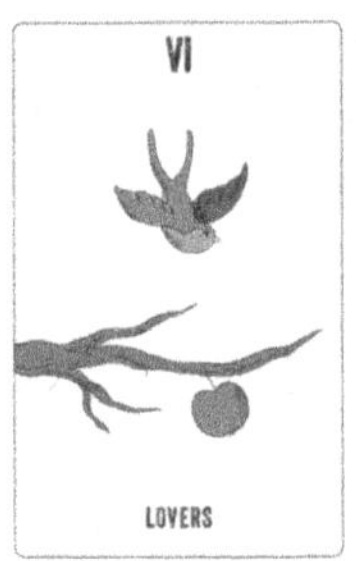

LOVERS: expansion, partnership, community, relationships, support, being seen, balance, freedom, self-discovery, choices, acceptance, experimentation, responsibility, caretaking

CHARIOT: seeking, quests, triumph, breaking boundaries, inquisition, courage, perseverance, finding meaning, determination, discovery, pride

STRENGTH: patience, wisdom, power, confidence, discipline, resilience, maturity, trusting in our own experience, momentum, being well-resourced and supported

HERMIT: spirituality, observation, care, authenticity, reflection, attention to detail, intentionality, philanthropy, stepping back from movement, release

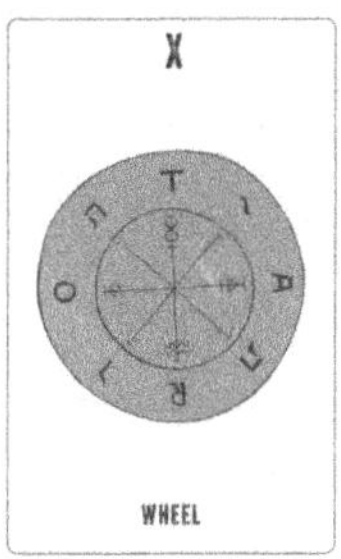

WHEEL: destiny, larger forces, control, change, movement, patterns, luck, cycles, transitions, trust, faith in something bigger, a new spark, timing

JUSTICE: collective crossroads, clarity, social structures, consequences, ideals, balance, seeking truth, equality, fairness, nuance, decision-making, problem-solving

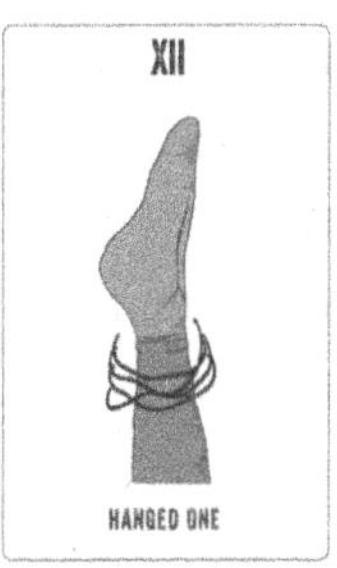

HANGED ONE: internal expansion, halted progress, surrender, sacrifice, truth, perspective, patience, discomfort, reflection, awareness, uncertainty, stillness

DEATH: natural order, loss, grief, an inevitable end, transformation, freedom, change, opportunities, releasing a burden, answers to old questions, relief

TEMPERANCE: awareness, coincidence, everyday magic, wonder, moderation, harmony, balancing tension, contradictions, clarity, optimism, possibility, integration

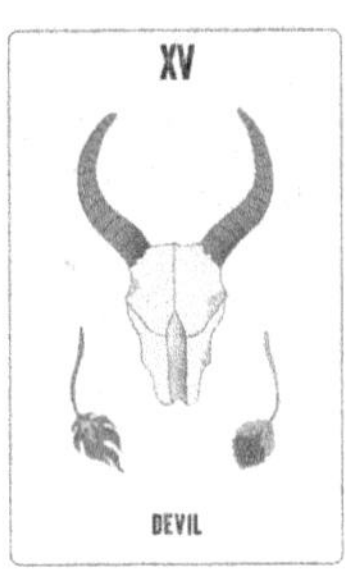

DEVIL: power, temptation, distraction, wildness, surrender, captivity, desire, cravings, old patterns, destructive habits, challenges, a longing for freedom, rebellion, authenticity

TOWER: forced assessment, chaos, lack of control, sudden change, rapid movement, freedom, experience, disruption, fear, confusion, release, destruction, adventure

STAR: internal power, hope, faith, healing, recovery, compassion, sovereignty, insight, clarity, reflection, steadiness, bravery, changing perspectives or new insights

MOON: strange wisdom, uncertainty, fears, dreams, exploration, fantasy, instinct, ferocity, introspection, illusion, embracing inner wildness, internal release

SUN: multiplying sparks, abundance, clarity, celebration, achievement, pride, acceptance, dignity, expression, unification, integration, laughter, joy, playfulness, lack of self-consciousness

JUDGEMENT: internal crossroads, forgiveness, awakening, compassion, release, evaluation, transformation, stepping out of a cycle, regeneration, confidence

WORLD: expansion of self, completion, stability, serenity, satisfaction, the knowledge that something is finished, tranquility, strength, fulfillment

Tarot decks also include the minor arcana, which is divided into four suits of fourteen cards each. Each of these suits includes ten pip cards, which are numbered one through ten, as well as four court cards. Where the major arcana tend to speak to more dramatic, impactful, or permanent events, the minor arcana are geared toward everyday life: the energies, relationships, decisions, struggles, victories, revelations, discoveries, and lessons that we all experience through the course of our lives, and sometimes just through the course of a single week.

While major arcana cards have a huge range of correspondences that have been developed, argued over, and added to over the centuries, minor arcana cards are each a combination of a number and an element. How you interpret each number and each element is again, wildly personal, but here are some tidbits to get you started:

The Elements

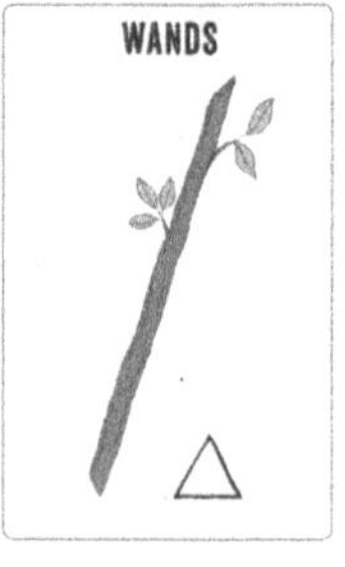

WANDS / FIRE: *driving force, movement, pursuit, willpower, desire, creativity, passion, the erotic*

SWORDS / AIR: *intellect, perception, truth, communication, information, analysis, logic*

CUPS / WATER: *emotional center, relationships, empathy, intuition, compassion, connections*

PENTACLES / EARTH: *physical and tangible, resources, sensation, embodiment, daily tasks*

The Numbers

1: *potential, power, sparks of an idea or desire or inspiration or insight, the beginning of a journey or pursuit, energy, imagination*

2: *choice, partnership, balance, awareness, planning, contemplation, observation, duality, harmony, attention, wisdom*

3: *tangible steps, manifestation, expression, progress, communication, being seen, collaboration, abundance, celebration*

4: *boundaries, foundations, rationality, structure, rules, steady effort, protection, stewardship, focus, legacy, traditions*

5: *change, uncertainty, friction, adventure, challenging norms, moving through obstacles, midpoints, a pivot or shift in direction*

6: *transition, finding harmony, leaving something challenging behind, nostalgia, relationships, community, reciprocity*

7: *assessment, seeking, discovery, awareness, adjustment, meaningful action, vision, purpose, questioning, acknowledgment*

8: *power, momentum, discipline, focus, intentionality, resources, abundance, success, movement, drive, achievement*

9: *independence, achievement, incoming change, approaching or achieving completion of a long-term goal or ambition*

10: *pushing the energy of the suit to its limit, celebration, preparing for a new beginning, rhythms and patterns, release*

The Court Cards

11 OR 2/ PAGE: *young and eager explorer, natural talent, innate trust, communication, insights, curiosity, questions, rebels*

12 or 3 / KNIGHT: *adolescense, potential, adventure, courage, action-oriented, stubbornness, ambition, focused mindset, unfinished ideas, taking chances*

13 or 4 / QUEEN: *internal leadership, guidance by example, artistic creators, compassionate and nurturing energy, sensitivity, emotional connections, personal transformation, collaborative creativity, inspiration, teachers, guides*

14 or 5 / KING: *external leadership, influence, authority, decisiveness, energy that causes others to listen and move into action, architects, community leaders, founders, changemakers, legacy builders, thinking of the collective*

• • •

When folks think about working with tarot cards, they usually imagine *reading* the tarot: asking a question, shuffling the deck, selecting a card (or series of cards), and interpreting them as answers or responses to the question posed. Tarot readers use the cards that have come up to tell a story and to make meaning based on their own experiences and studies. However, you can also work with tarot cards by choosing a specific card or cards to use in various ways: putting a card on an altar or shrine, using a card as a focus for meditation or spell, choosing cards to represent different characters or plot points, letting cards serve as inspiration for patterns or textures or flavors, or even physically following the movements suggested by the cards, just to name a few. Reading tarot is just *one* way to work with the cards.

When it comes to readings, different people have different beliefs about the cards and what they are capable of doing. I'm not here to tell you what the tarot means, either in a more general sense or in a specific card-based way: those things are for you to decide. But I will share my own beliefs about the cards with you, to offer some insights on my own approach as just one way of thinking through these ideas.

Personally, I believe that tarot cards can help us understand ourselves, our communities, and the world around us if we simply listen with honesty and courage. I tend to see any magic within the cards as coming from myself and whoever I'm reading for, but I can't pretend that there aren't times when it feels as if something greater is using the cards as a method of communication, that I'm tapping into something larger than myself. Sometimes I intentionally use the cards to commune with bigger energies or spirits, while other times I use them as a way to explore my own feelings and help me understand those hidden emotions, desires, or fears more clearly. I have also found tarot to be incredibly energizing when it comes to creative work. However you decide to use the cards, there's probably someone else out there doing something similar that you can learn from or be inspired by. And I think that's really fucking cool.

Where Did Tarot Come From?

Depending on whom you ask, tarot has either a very straightforward history or a deeply complicated and wildly unknowable history. (The truth probably lies somewhere in the middle.) The mythology around tarot is wide ranging, and while I personally am not particularly fussed about the nitty-gritty details of tarot's history, it can be helpful when diving into this practice to understand some basics about where the cards came from, how they've evolved, and whose history is most highly regarded.

As Rachel Pollack so wisely says in *A Walk through the Forest of Souls* (Weiser Books, 2023):

"The belief that [specific] meanings exist in the cards spurs people to find meanings the original designers may never have intended (please note: may never is not the same as never). Once found, however, those meanings exist, and the cards become a physical embodiment of a vast, organized, and coherent system of laws and structures. And once we have found (or constructed) that system in the images, the cards become an instrument of it." (37)

Everyone who has ever seen something in a tarot card, who writes about an archetype or shares their thoughts or develops a new set of correspondences, helps to co-create the myth of the card. The longer tarot cards are around, the more layered their meanings become—and that includes the history of this tool. Every group of occultists who saw meanings or mythologies within the cards, every scholar who found that they could use the cards for mysticism or divination or learning about kabbalah, every cultish group who worked to layer in meanings from Egyptian mythology or the Romani people—every one of these choices has led to the deck that we now have today.

Of course, there is not only one singular tarot deck. In fact, there are thousands, perhaps millions of different tarot decks—some indie creations, some singular works handmade by one artist, and some mass-produced for accessibility, all that serve as special and powerful tools for the people who wield them. But each tarot deck, no matter its style or tradition, contributes to the broader mystique of the cards themselves. Every time someone does a tarot reading with these cards, they add something to the beautiful mystery and wildly divergent perspectives on these cards.

While I'm not a tarot scholar or historian, enough other brilliant folks have shared their findings into the history of tarot that I feel comfortable covering some of the basics. Again, I do not think that it's essential to have an in-depth understanding of the complete history of tarot to read cards, but I do think that when navigating different perspectives on individual cards or considering where certain interpretations and ideas about tarot originated, having a general concept of history can be very helpful.

Playing cards and card games have existed in some iteration for centuries, but the earliest decks that resemble our modern-day tarot cards were created in the 1300s. Some say that these decks were used strictly for card games, pleasure, and play, but again, depending on your source, it's possible that these cards were used for divinatory purposes from the very beginning.

The best that historians can tell, the first versions of our modern tarot decks developed in Europe in the 1500s. Playing cards as well as Mamluk cards from Egypt were common objects at this point, and while the church railed against them loudly as "inventions of the Devil" (Roger J. Horne, *Cartomancy in Folk Witchcraft,* Moon Over the Mountain Press, 2022, 13), these cards were commonly used for gambling, games, and storytelling. While it can be difficult to parse exactly what the first "true" tarot deck is or to nail down exactly who may have designed it, we do know that the earliest tarot decks are distinguished by their use of the fifth suit as a trump suit, which was used to win tricks in card games (hence the origin of the word *trump* for these major arcana archetypes). These decks were often either hand-painted for wealthy families as treasured artistic objects or used for parlor games.

Some tarot histories claim that tarot cards weren't used for divination until centuries later, but it's important to remember that Europe in the 1500s included peoples from all of the world. While the Romani people who had migrated there used many different tools for predictions and fortune-telling, it's likely that they were the first to begin using both playing cards and tarot cards for divinatory purposes, and were actively doing so as tarot developed.

These earliest tarot decks differed from each other in many ways, with different trump cards, different numbers of trump cards, and different orders of the trump cards. As time went on and these cards spread in popularity, the Marseilles style of deck became standardized and eventually was printed in larger quantities by woodblock-style presses that are still creating the same decks today. These Marseilles-style decks, with their beautifully illustrated major arcana cards and simple, geometric minor arcana cards, are considered by many to be the oldest "traditional" tarot decks.

In the 1700s, several French occultists began to make unsubstantiated claims that tarot originated from Egypt rather than Europe, and contained hidden wisdom from Hermes Trismegistus, the Book of Thoth, Jewish kabbalah, and Egyptian mystics. But rather than doing this from any kind of attempt to offer respect or tribute to the Romani people for their contributions to the development of tarot as a divination tool, instead the main purpose of this claim seems to be exoticizing tarot to make it more enticing to the masses and to paint it as something worthy of in-depth study by those "in the know." These rumors were published in rather authoritative ways and became very mainstream, weaving into established tarot history so thoroughly that it's still difficult to separate fact from fiction in studying tarot's development today.

By the late 1800s, occultist groups were popping up all over Europe, seeking knowledge and claiming to have hidden insights into the uses of magic, tarot, alchemy, and other mysterious wisdom. The Hermetic Order of the Golden Dawn, leaning heavily on the teachings of the French occultists from the previous century, developed their own system of tarot correspondences, the most famous being their astrological correspondences that many still use. And two of their members, Arthur Edward (A. E.) Waite and Aleister Crowley, partnered with artists Pamela Colman Smith and Lady Frieda Harris to create their own tarot decks: the *Rider-Waite-Smith,* arguably the most popular tarot deck in history and still the most recognizable card illustrations today, and the *Thoth* deck, a more esoteric and layered card set that was published after Crowley's death.

The Rider-Waite-Smith deck, with its illustrated pip cards likely inspired by the Sola Busca deck from Italy in the 15th century, was illustrated by Pamela Colman Smith. While the cards were relatively successful on their initial publishing, they were republished in the 1970s and gained a lot of traction, becoming extremely popular and, for many people, serving as the "original" tarot cards and illustrations rather than the much older Marseilles pattern. Often abbreviated to RWS, this deck is arguably the most well known of the three tarot traditional decks and has been recreated and modernized thousands of times over the years.

The final tarot tradition to be aware of is Aleister Crowley's Thoth deck, illustrated by Lady Frieda Harris. This is easily the most visually complex card set, as it weaves in a wide variety of correspondences and can be a bit more difficult to read, in my experience. However, the folks who are into this deck absolutely love it and find a lot of value and depth within these illustrations, as well as Crowley's accompanying writings on the imagery.

After the publishing of the Thoth tarot, tarot readers and scholars began to push back against the notion that one had to be a lifelong magician devoted to the occult arts in order to read tarot. In the 1960s and 1970s, books and decks that were being published reasserted that the tarot trumps were archetypes and encouraged tarot readers to make their own meanings rather than simply repeating ones that had been previously established.

Today, tarot continues to enjoy a major resurgence, increasing in popularity by the year. Many of us sought spirituality outside of religion, others wanted a tool for self-reflection and self-discovery, and some simply wanted a creative and inspirational tool to use in personal or professional work. And, of course, there are always folks who are drawn to the cards because they are interested in magic, divination, and feeling a sense of control over their own destiny. Tarot has a very wide utility, making it a powerful system for anyone who is interested in working with it.

For transparency, my own tarot reading style is largely Marseilles-inspired, which means that I tend to lean on numerology and elements rather than keywords alone in my tarot interpretations. However, I usually try to include or honor the RWS interpretations as well, since these are the ones that most folks learn in the beginning of their tarot journey. I do not work with the Thoth deck in my personal practice, but you can find additional resources on working with it in the recommended resources section at the back of this book.

Who Can Read Tarot?

Tarot is for everyone.

It does not matter if you have years of experience with the tarot or are still considering whether or not to buy your first deck. It does not matter if you use lengthy and complicated tarot spreads or if you prefer general single-card readings. It does not matter if you read for others or if you read only for yourself. It doesn't even matter if you do readings at all: you might prefer to use tarot cards as creative prompts or to storyboard a novel or to inspire a meal. Tarot has endless uses, and they're not all connected to predictions or deep internal work. No matter what your relationship is with spirituality, transformation, or divination, there's a way to use tarot cards that will already fit into your life.

Tarot is not a closed practice, though certain iterations of card reading are specific to the Romani people and should not be co-opted or appropriated by those who are not members of those ethnicities. But standardized seventy-eight-card tarot decks are open to everyone who is interested in building a relationship with the cards and engaging with them respectfully, honoring the ways that they have developed and being open to new ways of learning about what the cards have come to mean.

If you want to work with the tarot, the tarot is for you.

How Does Tarot Work?

Ah, the million dollar question. Tarot "works" in mysterious ways.

By that I mean everyone's beliefs around tarot might be different. Some folks view the tarot as a reflection of self, a manifestation of our own internal perspectives, magic, and wisdom. There are also many who use tarot specifically as a tool to communicate with ancestors, spirits, deities, planets, or energies of the Other variety. Some use tarot as a channel for prayer with a specific god or set of gods. And still others view the deck itself as enshrined with power, believing that readings work by communing with the magic of the cards themselves.

You get to decide, for yourself, how you believe that tarot works. And before you dig into readings, I highly encourage you to spend some time thinking about this issue because it will impact how you view the truths that the cards reveal. Do you believe in free will or in fate? Do you believe that the cards can predict a future that is fixed or that tarot simply reveals a potential outcome based on your current trajectory? Do you intend to use your cards to forecast what will definitely happen? Do you believe that forecasts like that are possible?

There are no right or wrong answers here. And your beliefs may shift as you work with the cards more in depth. Sometimes people use the cards for creative inspiration and never consider reading them in a more divinatory style, whereas others primarily use the cards to try to predict the future and therefore act accordingly. Your beliefs can be your own. But before diving too deeply into a tarot practice, think about what your readings will mean to you and how you will understand them in the grand scheme of your rational mind, tender heart, instinctive spirit, and physical body. How does tarot fit into your worldview? And how will you make meaning of the cards that come forward for you in readings?

Something else to keep in mind, especially if you end up reading tarot for or with other people, is that their beliefs may differ from yours. That's okay! Ask questions and open up a dialogue around tarot beliefs, especially with folks you trust who may view their readings differently than you do. Don't make assumptions around tarot theologies. When in doubt, ask, and by encouraging your friends or clients to consider their own tarot beliefs, you will help them get clarity around readings too.

Can I Buy My Own Decks?

Absolutely, you can! For many folks, this is a joyful and exciting aspect of tarot.

Buying your own decks is completely fine. One of the most persistent myths around tarot is that your first deck must be gifted to you, but I'm here to tell you that I bought my first deck for myself and have never regretted it. Part of tarot not being a closed practice is that you do not need to be formally invited or initiated into working with the cards. You can just choose a deck you want, buy it, and begin working with it. If this feels like a particular hangup for you, allow me to offer you a gentle reframe: you can gift *yourself* your first tarot deck.

To address some other myths, rumors, and gatekeeping ideas around tarot: you do not need to store the cards, or read with them, in any particular way. It's okay if you don't keep them wrapped in silk. You don't have to own a million decks, or limit yourself to only one deck, and you don't have to start reading with any specific set of cards if you don't want to. You don't have to read tarot every day, every week, or even every month. You don't have to take a class, get certified, or become an expert in tarot history. You don't have to tell anyone you're working with the cards or read for other people.

This practice can be yours—whatever that means to you.

What Kind of Deck Should I Get?

As I've mentioned, there are thousands and thousands of different tarot decks available created by a multitude of artists with different life experiences, interpretations, and points of view. Many tarot resources will recommend starting your practice by learning with one of the main three decks that established various traditions and paved the way for other creators to follow in their footsteps—but I won't put such constraints on you. Follow your heart, and choose a deck that sings to you, with imagery you appreciate and card stock that feels good in your hands. It can be useful, however, to be aware of the various traditions that offer foundational imagery, symbolism, and meanings for many modern decks, so that as you begin developing a relationship with the cards, you know what kind of deck you're working with.

These three foundational traditions are known as the Tarot de Marseille, the Rider-Waite-Smith, and the Thoth tarot. Often when you purchase a contemporary illustrated deck, the deck creator will indicate that it follows the "system" of the Rider-Waite-Smith—or Marseilles, or Thoth—even though the imagery itself may be vastly different. Imagery has evolved—and rightly so—to move away from being strictly gendered and bearing the hallmarks of colonization or religious precepts, which means that even a deck that follows a particular system may have a very different vibe from the original illustrations. In other words, you truly can choose any deck you like, but knowing which tradition it fits into (or that it may not fit into any of these systems!) will help you know which resources to lean on in the future.

Tarot de Marseille

The *Tarot de Marseille,* created in 1709 and first printed by Pierre Madenié, is the oldest of the most popular "traditional" tarot decks and at the time of this writing is making something of a resurgence among modern tarot readers. This deck pattern includes imagery for all twenty-two major arcana trump cards, but the minor arcana cards are extremely simple, using colors and numbers to make them identifiable but not offering any additional storytelling elements that may guide the reader in any particular interpretive direction. Court cards are separated into kings and queens, depicted as men and women of the higher court, as well as the pages and knights, who are members of the lesser court. Marseilles-style decks use illustrated trump cards and repeated patterns in the minor arcana and are wonderful for readers who want to focus on numerology, elements, and color theory in their readings. Most decks that were printed and distributed prior to the 1900s were made in some version of this style. Modern Marseilles decks that I recommend include *The Gay Marseille* by Charlie Claire Burgess, *Le Tarot de L'étoile Cachée* by Elisa Seitzinger, and *Metanoia Marseille* by Kerri Snook.

Rider-Waite-Smith

The Rider-Waite-Smith deck, created in 1909 by Arthur Edward Waite and illustrated by Pamela Colman Smith, uses specific images for the minor arcana cards to define one particular interpretation for every card in the deck. While the Sola Busca tarot was the earliest deck we still have copies of to illustrate all fifty-six minor arcana cards in addition to vivid depictions of the major arcana, and served as inspiration for Smith's own illustrations, the Rider-Waite-Smith pack introduced astrological correspondences that were created by the Hermetic Order of the Golden Dawn and was developed specifically with divination work in mind. The deck did moderately well when first published, but it experienced a surge in popularity in the 1970s when U.S. Games Systems began reprinting copies and made them more widely available for distribution. The Rider-Waite-Smith pack, and decks inspired by its illustrations and interpretations, is still the most recognizable tarot deck (and deck style) in the world. Rider-Waite-Smith style decks use standardized keywords and meanings for each card in the minor arcana, exploring these definitions through various lenses, and are often recommended to beginners because there are many resources available for this style of deck. Modern Rider-Waite-Smith decks that I recommend include the *Modern Witch Tarot* by Lisa Sterle, the *Muse Tarot* by

Chris-Anne Donnelly, and the *Queer Tarot* by Ashley Molesso and Chess Needham.

Thoth Tarot

The Thoth tarot, created in 1943 by Aleister Crowley and illustrated by Lady Frieda Harris, is probably the least popular of these "traditional" decks but has a devoted and loyal following nonetheless. Based on esoteric visions and dreams experienced by both Crowley and Harris, this deck uses art deco–style paintings, Egyptian mythology, and many layers of correspondences to offer a new perspective on each card. While potentially less accessible for beginners than the other two styles due to its complex imagery, the Thoth tarot is wonderful for Crowley enthusiasts or for any readers who are interested in incorporating kabbalah, astrology, alchemy, numerology, or Crowley's *The Book of the Law* into their readings. This deck is less frequently modernized than the other two main styles, so for those interested in working with it, I recommend picking up the original deck with Harris's illustrations.

Today, there are thousands and thousands of different tarot decks available. Many follow the three traditions that I've mentioned here, but artists are also branching out beyond these traditions, creating systems that feel entirely fresh and new. For those who would prefer something informed by but still fairly distinct from these traditions, I recommend the *Next World Tarot* by Cristy C. Road, *The Rosebud Tarot* by Diana Rose Harper and Amanda Lee Stilwell, and *The Spacious Tarot* by Carrie Mallon and Annie Ruygt.

When it comes to buying your first tarot deck, or choosing a new one, give yourself time and trust your instincts. There are many different styles of imagery and illustration, with every artist bringing something new to the cards. If you're not sure where to start, go to a bookstore to browse decks in person, ask friends or community members about their preferred decks, or explore the #tarot and #decklust hashtags on social media platforms. Start bookmarking or saving the decks that appeal to you, and pay attention to any commonalities. If you find that you continue to gravitate toward the same deck, do some research on it, and check out images for both the major and minor arcana along with the court cards. Don't make the mistake of just looking at the trump cards—the whole deck matters! Pay attention as well to the size, shape, and thickness of the cards. If you have smaller hands, oversized decks or thick card stock might be harder for you to shuffle. If you travel a lot, a deck with a sturdy box or a smaller size might be more convenient. And if you have trouble reading very small text, a larger deck or one with a clearer, bolder typeface might be easier for you to work with.

Remember too that digital tarot decks are an option and work just as well as physical decks. Whether you don't have space in your home, want to keep your tarot work private, have trouble shuffling, or just prefer an online experience, there are apps for your phone as well as websites that will allow you to explore decks, perform readings, and even read collaboratively with other people.

Let me gently warn you that buying tarot decks can be a slippery slope, so my personal recommendation is to choose a single deck to start with, and make it your primary set of cards to learn on. By building a relationship with one deck first and getting to know it well, you can focus on the meanings themselves rather than getting lost in various interpretations by different artists, scholars, or teachers. Whatever system you choose, there is plenty to uncover, and you can always introduce additional decks or tarot traditions into your practice as you grow your relationship with the cards.

How Do I Start Learning Tarot?

I have only two hard-and-fast rules for tarot:

> *Rule one: Do no harm. Tarot readings are vulnerable experiences and should never be used to manipulate, coerce, frighten, or control another person. That includes you! The tarot is not meant to be a tool for inflicting pain; it should be used with respect, compassion, and authenticity. Period.*
>
> *Rule two: Be consistent. Starting any practice includes some experimentation and learning curves, especially when it comes to basics like choosing a deck, shuffling the cards, selecting the cards for your reading, deciding if you're going to use reversals, and interpreting the cards. But once you start to figure out what feels good for you in terms of working with the cards, be as consistent as possible about that practice. Consistency will help you trust your readings, and trust yourself.*

The best way to learn tarot is to get yourself a deck and start working with it. Tarot is a language that takes time to learn, so there really aren't any shortcuts beyond understanding the structure of the deck and building a relationship with your cards. Be patient with yourself, and don't rush the process. While there are plenty of "learn tarot quick" type tools out in the world, I have found that the best way to develop a tarot practice that actually sticks is by moving slowly, letting the deck speak to you, and learning in the style that best suits your brain and heart.

This is just my own opinion and methodology, but I believe that the process of learning tarot can be broken down into four main aspects: *memorization, comprehension, utilization,* and *relationship*. You can work with whichever of these aspects you like, in whatever order you prefer, but I think it's helpful to break down what learning tarot really means and to consider how we move from being able to rattle off keywords to being in full relationship with the deck.

Memorization is the point at which most people begin their tarot learning journey, and this includes learning to associate certain keywords and correspondences with specific cards. *Comprehension* is when layers of card meanings begin to emerge more organically, based on the keywords and correspondences that have been internalized, and a fuller understanding of the context and function of each card comes into play. *Utilization* goes further; it represents understanding which messages can be derived from the meanings that are being defined—in other words, being able to actually engage with the cards in a way that feels more flexible, expanding our awareness of what kinds of moments each card can speak to. And the fullest stage, *relationship*, is the ability to listen and internalize and communicate with the deck in a way that can have a tangible impact on your life, the skill to lean on both learned information and internal intuition to hear what the cards are communicating in readings, studies, magic, and other tarot practices.

With seventy-eight cards in the deck, feeling as though you have to memorize every card's meaning at once can be a little overwhelming, so I typically recommend instead starting slow and getting to know the cards, one by one. That is, begin with *comprehension* and context rather than jumping headfirst into *memorization*. For me, having an understanding of the correspondences of the cards aids heavily with learning their meanings and allows beginning tarot readers to immediately develop connections between the cards instead of thinking of them as seventy-eight separate ideas.

Many tarot teachers, myself included, recommend implementing a card-a-day practice, which is basically exactly what it sounds like: drawing one card every day (or once a week or whatever your schedule allows) and seeing what it might have to offer. These *can* be full tarot readings where you ask the deck what you need to know for that day, see what comes up, and interpret the card as a divinatory practice. But you can also just systematically work your way through every card in the deck, studying the images on each card, noting any keywords or definitions that come up, and considering each card's function in the broader cycle or story.

There are many, many different meanings for each card, so many that you may find tarot resources that contradict one another or disagree on what a card, suit, number, or archetype indicates. Some decks, especially ones with detailed illustrations, might offer highly specific interpretations of each card. Others may be more simple, minimal, or neutral, making space for readers to bring in their own experiences with the cards. Beginning with *comprehension* rather than prioritizing *memorization* allows you to slow down and relieve some of the pressure of "knowing" everything there is to know about a card. It takes a bit longer, but this approach allows you to start practicing listening and observing, to pay attention to not only what the card might mean but also what it might have to say, to teach, to offer as wisdom.

But, of course, your tarot journey is your own! No matter how you choose to learn the cards, be patient and keep going. The longer you work with the tarot, and the more you engage with tarot writings, readings, and studies, the more meanings will reveal themselves.

How Do I Do a Tarot Reading for Myself?

There are many ways to do a tarot reading for yourself or for someone else. And there are plenty of ways to describe this process. However, for me, the basic format of performing a tarot reading, whether using a tarot spread or doing a more open-ended reading, follows three main steps, which I've broken down in my preferred language here:

Step one: *Define what the reading will be about.* Before you pull any cards, get clear with yourself about what your tarot reading is going to focus on. Consider what it is you hope to receive from the cards or what you hope to accomplish with this reading. This contemplation can crystalize into a general question like "What do I need to know today?" or "What do I need to know right now?" It can also be more specific and focus on a particular concern, topic, situation, theme, or decision. *General readings,* or *open readings,* are labels that I personally use to describe tarot readings that don't use a specific tarot spread to guide the reading. But whether or not you're using a spread, it's important to hold in your mind what you are going to be pulling cards about so that you can interpret the reading accordingly—or to recognize when you're looking for more open-ended guidance.

Some people refer to this process as *setting an intention for the reading.* This part of the process is really about clarifying what you want from the cards and communicating to the cards what you want to talk about. Some readings will be much broader and more general, simply opening a door to a specific topic but leaving the conversation plenty of room to meander in whatever direction it wants to go. Other readings might be highly specific with very detailed or nuanced questions being presented to the cards. Both work well, depending on what you're looking for. This process is important whether or not you're using a tarot spread as part of your reading.

Whether you're using a spread or pulling cards in a more free-form manner, I like to think about tarot readings as conversations with your cards. Just as when you talk to a friend, sometimes you might just reach out to chat, catch up, or check in. But other times you might reach out specifically hoping for advice or insights from them, craving another perspective, or perhaps even seeking your friend's help in making a decision. You can approach the tarot and tarot readings in the exact same way—either looking to say hello and gain some open-ended perspective or to ask a particular question and receive support.

Either way, think closely about what you want to talk to the tarot about *before* you start pulling cards out of the deck, and your reading will go much more smoothly.

Step two: *Shuffle and draw cards for your reading.* There are many different ways to shuffle your tarot cards. I tend to alternate between riffle shuffling and overhand shuffling, but you can also mix the cards loosely together on a flat surface or even develop your own technique based on your needs and preferences. Regardless of the method you choose, remember that shuffling is really just an opportunity to mix up the cards well, cleanse any energy that might be hanging out in your cards from a previous reading, and meditate on what you are asking the cards about. You don't need to do any fancy shuffling techniques in order to blend the cards together for your reading. You also don't have to always shuffle for the same amount of time or do a certain kind of shuffle the same number of times (although some folks like to be very consistent with their shuffling, and that's absolutely okay too!). I tend to just shuffle the cards until they feel ready, which has come with practice, awareness, and time. There are not hard-and-fast rules for shuffling beyond making sure the cards are well mixed.

The process of drawing specific cards for your reading after you've shuffled them is similar in that there are many different ways to do it, and there's no right or wrong way to choose the cards that you're going to read. Once the cards are well shuffled, my personal method is to cut the deck into three stacks, then consolidate them into one full stack, and finally draw the cards for my reading from the top of the pile. Some people choose cards only from the middle of the stack, and others read only the cards that are on the bottom of the deck. You can spread your cards out in a line or in a pool on the table and draw from there. Or you can read cards that "jump," meaning cards that fall or pop out of the deck while you're shuffling. It's entirely up to you.

I stated earlier that consistency is important in tarot, and this is one of the areas where consistency really does make a difference. As you're learning to shuffle the cards and developing your own tarot rituals, you should absolutely experiment with different methods to see what feels good and what works best for you. Once you've settled into a routine that works for you, be as consistent about that routine as possible. It's okay if your habits are different for different decks, or if you use a different method when reading for another person than you do when reading for yourself. Consistency makes it easier for you to trust your reading process, to trust the cards, and ultimately, to trust yourself. For example, if you read the cards that jump out of the deck only when you see that the fallen card is one that you're really excited about, how can you really judge any accuracy in your readings? Do yourself a favor and build in consistency from the beginning, and it will make developing an authentic and affirming relationship with your tarot cards much easier.

Step three: *Read the cards.* Once you've clarified what you're looking for from your tarot reading, shuffled the deck, and drawn cards, all that's left to do is actually complete the reading. Depending on how many cards you've chosen and what the topic is, this step can take anywhere from a couple of minutes to a couple of hours. Sometimes, a tarot reading won't fully click into focus for days, weeks, or even years later, so be patient with yourself.

There are many different methods for actually reading the cards: from using the little white book that came with your deck or other tarot resources to entirely relying on your intuition to studying imagery, colors, shapes, keywords, narratives, cycles, numerology, elements, astrology, or other correspondences, among other things. Reading tarot is a very personal matter, and everyone has a slightly different and unique method for doing so, which is part of what makes working with the tarot so special.

Whether I'm doing single-card readings or multi-card readings, my process is essentially the same: I begin by assessing what the cards themselves are, which sometimes may take a moment if you're using a deck that's unfamiliar to you or one that has different names or glyphs from the ones you initially learned. (This is where hanging on to the guidebook that comes with your deck can come in very handy, even if you don't use it for every reading!) Then, I look at the general correspondences that I work with, namely the number associated with the card and sometimes the element or astrological connection. Those correspondences often help to bring specific keywords, definitions, and meanings to the surface, and I will take some time to consider how those correspondences might feel relevant. The final step, and sometimes the trickiest, is to recognize which of these meanings or ideas best answers the question that I brought to the cards in the first place. And if I find myself feeling completely lost on what the cards are trying to communicate, then I'll look to resources from tarot writers and teachers that I trust, to see if their writings or ideas around the cards help to offer clarity or unlock something in my own intuition.

You may find that you prefer to jump straight to meanings, that correspondences are more frustrating than helpful for you, or that your intuition is very loud and immediately pops in with something for you to pay attention to. You may prefer to do automatic writing, meditation, prayer, or movement to help get your intuitive juices flowing. You may also like to look at other resources earlier in the process than I do. There really isn't a right or wrong way to do this—simply *your* way. Your personal methodology for reading will develop as you go, so try out different techniques and see what makes the most sense for you.

If you're into journaling or recording your rituals, keeping track of your tarot readings as you go (especially longer or more emotionally intense readings) can be an incredible way to develop your practice and trace short- or long-term patterns, recall personal histories, and observe cycles of transformation. Sometimes a reading that seems clear in the moment will later take on a completely different significance, and the beautiful thing is both of those readings can still be fully accurate! Hindsight may change the ways that we understand a message, so anytime you can record your readings even with a quick snapshot on your phone or a scribbled note in your tarot grimoire, I highly recommend doing so.

If you're just getting started with the cards, reading tarot may feel confusing, frustrating, or hard to do. Please rest assured that this is absolutely normal. Reading tarot can be really difficult! It takes time, practice, devotion, patience, and curiosity to become fluent with the cards, so keep at it. Record your readings, even if you aren't completely sure what they mean. Be gentle with yourself as you learn this new, complicated thing. Enjoy the process rather than rushing toward the finish line. And keep asking questions, even if the answers take time to reveal themselves.

What If I Have More than One Question for My Cards?

In general, I encourage you to do separate and distinct tarot readings for different topics, rather than trying to cram multiple broad questions into one larger reading. If you have a question about a romantic relationship but are also curious about a new creative project, each situation could likely benefit from its own tarot reading. Unless they are directly connected, I do not suggest doing one big reading that examines both in depth. The exception would be a spread that has a position or two for various aspects of life: For example, a spread that specifically looks at emotional, relational, spiritual, physical, and intellectual aspects of self could explore many topics at once through a more general lens.

However, when you have multiple questions about one particular aspect of your life, like your job, health, relationships, community, spirituality, creativity, or a decision (to name just a few), this is where a tarot spread can be incredibly helpful, and what we'll be covering throughout the rest of this book.

As an alternative to single-card readings or reading with spreads, you can also use a more casual, conversational technique when reading cards for yourself. If you start by pulling a few cards around a specific topic but find that you are craving clarity, deeper insights, advice, or something else that doesn't show up in the initial reading, you can pull additional cards one at a time, asking specific questions and then pulling cards as a response to those questions.

For example, say you wanted to do a general reading on making a decision. A new creative opportunity has come up, and you're trying to assess your own feelings about it, to understand if it's something that you want to do or not. You ask the cards for some general insights on this opportunity and pull three cards that feel encouraging, supportive, and positive. Yet you still feel a pang of uncertainty, like there's more to uncover. You could certainly put all of the cards back in the deck, reshuffle, and do a completely new reading with different questions about the same topic. Or you could tell your deck that you have some additional questions and pull more cards.

I like to do this one card at a time, since sometimes you need only a card or two to clarify or expand the reading before the meaning becomes clear. General questions you can try include

- Can you tell me more about this specific card?
- What else might I need to know?
- What's the next step I should take?
- What can I do right now to reach my desired result?
- What should I be careful of?
- What question should I be asking of myself?

In the case of our specific example on decision-making, some more questions might be

- What am I missing?
- Where is my uncertainty coming from?
- How can I feel more secure in what I'm seeing?
- What obstacle is tripping me up right now?

As with any reading, move slowly with your interpretations, and resist the urge to pull a dozen cards at once. This technique is meant to add clarity, so if you find yourself getting even more confused, pulling more cards is unlikely to help. Grab some water, take a break, and come back to the cards later with a clearer perspective.

How Do I Read Tarot *with* Another Person?

No matter your experience level, reading tarot with another person or with a group of people can be a fun and extremely educational experience. Reading alongside folks you trust is a great way to learn the tarot, but it also can be a joyful and thought-provoking way to expand your own understanding of the cards. It can even challenge your notions of certain cards, especially if you tend to get stuck on certain archetypes or always read a particular card in the same way. And if you're someone who is just getting started in a tarot practice, this can be an affirming and supportive way to explore the cards that feels quite different from practicing readings on your own. If you're interested in expanding your practice and engaging with the tarot in a new way, group tarot readings are an easy way to do so.

The idea here is fairly simple: rather than one person serving as the primary reader and shuffling, pulling, and reading cards for one other person, *everyone* who participates gets to contribute their own thoughts, feelings, ideas, and interpretations into the reading. While you can do group tarot readings with any number of people at any skill level, I recommend keeping the group fairly small so that no one gets too overwhelmed and so that everyone gets a chance to speak. The more frequently you do this practice, the easier and more natural it will become. And if you read consistently with the same people, you will all develop your skills alongside one another, which can be incredibly satisfying in the long term.

There are a few ways to go about this approach, but as with any tarot reading, I recommend figuring out what (and whom) you're reading for before you begin pulling cards. Will this reading apply for everyone present? Are you pulling for a broader community at large or for others who may not be physically with you? Are you all providing support or encouragement or advice for one specific person who is there? Get real about what the reading is about and whom it's for, and either choose a spread to use or decide together how many cards you'll be pulling.

You can have one person designated as the shuffler, who mixes up the cards and selects a few based on their own tarot reading practice. Or each person who is participating in the reading can take turns shuffling before the cards are ultimately selected. If everyone wants to be involved, one person can spread the cards out on the flat surface in a line or in a messy pool, and each person can choose a card that will be part of the reading. However you go about this process, make sure everyone is on the same page!

Once the cards have been selected, the real fun begins. You can go around in a circle or can just begin a more free-form conversation, but give everyone involved a chance to share their thoughts and interpretations. I find it helpful with these collaborative readings to encourage everyone to share what comes to mind at first glance—not to necessarily stress about interpreting the card right away, but to just have a conversation about what each person sees in the card or cards. Keep the original question or situation in mind, and talk through how the cards drawn might serve as a response to that question.

When pulling multiple cards or reading a spread as a group, I prefer to collectively go through the reading one card at a time rather than looking at the full grouping of cards right away. This method makes it easier to keep the conversation relatively focused, especially if a large number of cards were pulled. Once each card has been examined on its own, you can discuss the entire reading together. But you might also like to just let each person share their general impressions based on the entire group of cards, rather than going through each card individually. Feel it out, and see how folks like to do their readings.

Sometimes deciding when the reading is finished can be tricky when you have multiple people involved! Make sure everyone has had a chance to speak and weigh in, and if the reading was for a particular person who is present, check in with them to see if they felt that their question was answered or if they still have any confusion about the reading.

Reading with a group can take practice, especially if you have folks with very different reading styles. But if you've never read with a group, definitely give it a try. You will almost certainly learn something, not just about the tarot but also about the folks you are reading with.

How Do I Read Tarot *for* Another Person?

Pulling tarot cards for someone else is a big responsibility and can be a very intimate experience. I do not suggest reading tarot for another person until you can confidently read for yourself, even if the other person is not paying you for this service. There's a lot of vulnerability in having your cards read, and even with a question that seems lighthearted, it's very easy to slip into much more serious topics, traumas, or emotions. Use a lot of care when reading for other people, and make sure you take your time, read with compassion, and don't just use the cards to share your own advice. Reading tarot for another person can mean serving as a translator for them, an open channel between the wisdom of the cards and the person you're reading for. Don't ever use the tarot to manipulate, coerce, confuse, or control anyone else.

When you're reading tarot for another person, it's very important that you have a clear understanding of what the querent is asking. Just like when you're reading for yourself, take your time and ask plenty of questions so that you can hone in on what the querent is really looking for from the cards. Let the person share as much with you as they like, work with them to narrow down their overall question, and be sure that you're both on the same page about what the reading will be about before you start to draw cards.

Some people like to have the querents shuffle and pull cards themselves, while others prefer to be the only person who handles their own tarot deck. Both are completely acceptable ways to read for another person and are simply a matter of personal preference. Be clear with the person you're reading for on this expectation so that no one gets embarrassed or frustrated about who is handling the cards.

After you are both clear on what the reading will be, what it will be about, and whether or not a spread will be used, take your time shuffling, breathing, and drawing the cards. Don't rush or get in your head about being observed. It's normal to have some nerves, but remember that you are the one guiding the reading. It can go at whatever pace is comfortable for you.

Once the cards are drawn, I tend to talk through what I see as the meanings of each card first, and then I speak to how the cards might answer the questions posited by the querent. Some readers like to be the only ones who share their perspective, but I take a collaborative approach and usually ask the person I'm reading for what they see in the cards after I've shared my initial impressions. Sometimes the cards will bring up details or topics that didn't seem relevant at first but turn out to be connected in a way that only the querent may know. Other times, you or the querent may be a bit stumped as to how a card might be relevant to the reading, and in those cases, talking it through together can often illuminate an important meaning or a different perspective that is useful to remember and can give more nuance to the reading.

Again, in multi-card readings I tend to move through each card individually first and then conclude by looking at the cards as a whole. But you might prefer to start with a more general set of observations about the entire group of cards and may then get more granular by going through each card one by one. Whatever practices you have developed by reading for yourself, utilize them in the same way when reading for someone else. This isn't the time to try out a fancy new technique or reading style! Stick with what you know, and save the experimentation for your solo practice—that is, of course, unless the querent is aware of what you're testing and fully consents to something that you're in the process of learning. Sometimes it's easier to test a new technique or skill for someone else, but don't try this unless the person you're reading for is well aware of what's going on.

My best reminders for reading for other people are to go slow, be compassionate, and listen, both to the cards and to the querent. Remember that tarot can bring up sensitive topics and that querents are often putting themselves into a vulnerable position during readings, so be as kind as possible, even if the cards bring up messages or answers that are difficult. Remember too that the purpose of reading for another person is to center their question, needs, and safety—not to prove what a badass tarot reader you are or how many card meanings you know.

What If I Don't Understand My Reading?

I can't stress enough just how normal it is to pull cards and not know immediately what they mean, either in general or in response to your question. Whether you're just getting started or have been reading for years, every single tarot reader I know has had a time when they pulled cards and have not understood what the fuck the cards are trying to tell them. There can be a few different reasons for this.

Often, this issue comes up when we are too close to the thing that we're asking about to clearly understand what the cards are trying to communicate. If you're looking at the cards and breathing hard, heart in your throat, desperate for assurance or guidance, it can be really hard to listen clearly or to be able to take in the messages you're receiving. In this case, I highly recommend either having a friend redo the reading for you or just consulting with them to see if they can help you make sense of the reading. If the topic of your reading is really tender, really vulnerable, or really scary or important, talking it through with someone you trust can help you find a different perspective. This challenge is why even professional tarot readers get readings from other tarot professionals! Some things are simply too hard to read objectively on our own, no matter how experienced of a tarot reader you are.

Not understanding your reading can also happen when the question isn't particularly clear. If you're shuffling your cards, asking a dozen questions at the same time, or pulling cards while still clarifying what it is you actually want to know, the deck can get confused about what you're looking for. This is why it's important to clarify what you want from the cards *before* you start drawing cards. In this instance, I recommend putting the cards away and doing something completely different, not attempting the reading again until few hours or even a few days later. I don't suggest immediately trying to do another reading on the same topic, as this can get a bit muddy when the new reading inevitably contradicts your first reading. Instead, take your time to really reckon with what it is you're looking for from the cards and to clarify one specific question that you want to explore. You may also want to use this time to research different spreads you could use for the reading.

There are plenty of other reasons that a tarot reading might be confusing, but the last one I'll mention here is that sometimes we don't understand our readings because we're trying to use a card meaning that simply doesn't make sense. Some tarot learning methods focus exclusively on memorizing keywords or "universal meanings" for the cards. And while this approach can be really handy as an initial introduction to tarot, it can quickly create problems when the one word you use for a card doesn't seem to make sense for the question you brought to your reading. If this is regularly happening for you, it is a great opportunity to expand your perspective on the card or cards you're struggling with. Use a little white book, grab your favorite tarot resource, or phone a friend, and go beyond the initial definition that you've got. Pay attention to numerological or elemental correspondences. Consider more expansive meanings beyond what you first learned. Not only can this method help to clarify the reading you're currently working through, but it will also show you some deeper definitions for your cards. Tarot cards have so many meanings—yes, even the pips!—so it's worth taking time to do deeper dives into individual cards to see what other definitions, keywords, and correspondences you can discover.

Now, I want to stress here that this is not a suggestion to try to find alternative meanings to cards simply because you don't like what the tarot has told you! This method is for moments of genuine confusion. If you're asking the deck for guidance, clarity, affirmation, or advice, but you internally know that you're only going to be happy with one kind of answer, a tarot reading is probably not going to be particularly constructive. (For example, if you're pulling cards for advice on how to deal with a crush, knowing full well that you've already decided to make a move regardless of what the cards may share, either put the deck away or come up with a more honest question. If you've already made a decision, why are you asking for advice? Is there something else you could use instead, or is tarot not really the tool for this particular moment?) Regardless of what other advice you may follow or what other exercises you may use to interpret your reading, take your time. Confusing readings happen to everybody, and rushing the process to get an answer as quickly as possible rarely helps provide clarity. Give yourself space, leave the cards out, and take a break or journal through it. Tarot isn't something that needs to be rushed.

What's the Deal with Tarot Reversals?

With the exception of circular tarot cards, which have their own more elaborate system, most tarot imagery has an upright position as well as a reversed, or upside-down, position. I am an English-speaking person who lives in the United States, so for me, a card is generally upright when I can read any words or numbers as written, moving from left to right. Depending on which language you speak and what your cards look like, it is sometimes more complicated to deduce if a card is upright or reversed on first glance. Generally, if the writing or imagery of a card is upright, that's the "standard" way to view it, and if the card is upside-down, it's considered reversed.

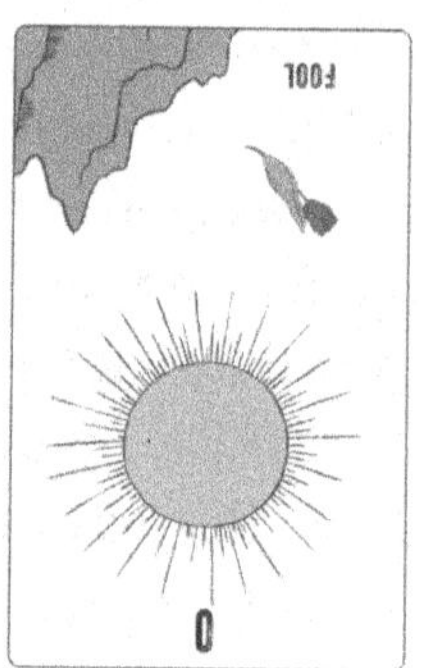

Reversals are a reading technique that includes noticing any cards that come out of the deck when pulled upside-down in that drawn position, and allowing that change in position to impact the way that the card is interpreted. Reversals are entirely optional, but if you decide to read with them, it's important to do so with consistency.

There are several different ways to read tarot reversals. One of the most common ways to read reversals is as an inverted meaning or an opposite meaning. This could be considered a shadow meaning or a contrasting meaning. In this way readers who use this technique are essentially doubling the number of potential meanings in a deck and expanding the ways that each card can be viewed. When a card comes up reversed using this technique, it invites in an alternative meaning to the one used when the card is upright. So, for example, if the Magician indicates imagination and possibility and anticipating a new journey in its upright position, the Magician reversed might speak to an internal blockage, feeling stuck or uncertain, or doubting our ability to move in a new direction.

Another way to read reversals is to view any reversed cards that come up in a reading as pertaining to an obstacle or a challenge for the querent. Whether you're using a tarot spread or not, if a card shows up reversed, it might serve as a call to action, or an indication to you that this is an important card to work with. So to continue with our Magician example, when we use this technique, the Magician reversed might instead mean that we need to make a lot of space for brainstorming and trailblazing, and take intentional time to tap into this archetype's expansive and courageous energy.

One final popular way to work with reversals is simply seeing reversed cards as having extra emphasis in a reading—or serving as a kind of exclamation point. This method does not include changing the meaning of the cards but instead is a way for the deck to indicate that this card is particularly important to pay attention to or a card that has a lesson or theme that is important for the reading as a whole. The Magician would still hold all of its usual meanings; it would just be particularly important for the overall flow of the meaning, like it's bolded and underlined.

There are certainly many other methods and ways of reading reversals, as this is a popular technique that can be used in a number of different ways. Personally, I do not read reversals, which is why I do not have a robust set of teachings on this technique. If you're interested in working with reversals or incorporating them into your practice, I recommend *The Complete Book of Tarot Reversals* by Mary K. Greer.

What Else Can I Do with Tarot Cards?

Beyond readings, tarot cards can serve as inspiration, support, or focus for nearly anything you can imagine. Entire books are written about this very topic (including a separate section of my first book, *Finding the Fool*), so I won't spend too much time on this subject here—but I will offer just a few brief suggestions.

If you are a writer or artist, tarot can be an incredible tool for developing characters, organizing a series, digging into conflict, navigating relationships, mapping out a narrative, and identifying themes. If you work with food or fragrance, tarot cards can help you explore flavors and scents, offer inspiration for new meals, or suggest unexpected pairings for something new. If you create music or poetry, you may find that tarot has a rhythm all its own, one that the cards can help you play within to develop beautiful harmonies or sharp, truthful insights. If you're someone who crafts, using fabric or yarn or clay or stone or some other medium to create something new for beauty or function, the cards have plenty to offer in terms of textures, shapes, movements, and colors. If you're a gamer, tarot can be a fantastic way to build worlds, create characters, flesh out conflicts or details, or write a compelling backstory. The sky's the limit!

Tarot is also wonderful to use in groups, with a partner, or in therapy. As a conversation starter, support with understanding events or emotions, or even just a tool for playful exploration, tarot can help us communicate ideas, delve into truths, or express things when words become challenging.

Beyond creativity and expression, if you are spiritual or religious, work with ancestors of any kind, enjoy meditation, use spellwork or mantras or prayers, or could otherwise use a specific energy or archetype as a focus, choosing individual tarot cards to work with or place on your altar can be a powerful invocation. Amateurs or professionals in various fields like astrology, herbalism, numerology, or mediumship can benefit greatly from the language of tarot, particularly during client work or research.

Some tarot cards are connected to specific modalities, like astrology, numerology, mythology, folklore, herbalism, elements, kitchen witchery, animal magic, and more. In this way, the cards can serve many other purposes beyond readings and can be incredibly useful if you are eager to learn more about a new topic or explore something in more depth. If you're already familiar with tarot, these more expansive decks can help provide a framework for new understanding, giving you information within a structure that already feels comfortable and familiar. If instead you're learning tarot but are well versed in a particular modality, choosing a deck to start with that includes correspondences connected to that modality can help you develop a deeper relationship to the cards right off the bat.

These are just a few suggestions to get you started. There are endless paths forward when it comes to tarot. And the more you get to know the cards, the more uses you may find for them.

Do I Have to Cleanse My Cards? What Does That Even Mean?

Cleansing your deck is an energetic technique that some people perform religiously, others do sparingly, and still others never complete at all. It's a very personal practice and is not required for all readers or for every reading—but cleansing can be helpful if you're using a deck that once belonged to someone else, that you haven't used in a while (or that has been getting a workout with a lot of readings), or that you use to read for other people.

There are dozens of ways to energetically cleanse your cards, and many of them are not particularly complicated. I like to light incense and wave the deck through the smoke, but you can also store the cards with a piece of clear quartz, leave them out overnight under the light of the new or full moon, or knock firmly on your deck as you would knock on a door. Some folks use bells or gongs to clear the energetic space around the deck, whereas others use candle smoke, cleansing sprays, or specific herbs. Please keep in mind that unless you have a specific cultural heritage, it's not necessary (and is in fact harmful) to engage with cultural appropriation by using a specific herb like white sage or palo santo. I often use stick incense from my local bodega for cleansing my cards and my spaces, and it works just fine.

Again, cleansing is entirely optional. There are folks who cleanse their cards every time they read and others who just do so after a particularly intense or deep reading. Listen to your intuition and develop a practice that feels right and makes sense for you.

Do I *Have* to Use a Tarot Spread in My Readings?

Ironically, given the title and subject of this book, the answer to this question is *no*. You absolutely do not have to use a tarot spread for your readings or in your tarot work in general. We'll talk more about the why and how of using tarot spreads in the rest of the book, but let me assure you right here at the beginning that if you are not interested in using tarot spreads, they are absolutely not mandatory for true, powerful, and revelatory tarot readings.

However, if you are interested in learning more about reading, writing, or revising tarot spreads, you're in the right place. Read on.

Anything Else I Should Know?

Becoming fluent in the language of tarot takes time, patience, attention, and a willingness to be honest with yourself. Regardless of how you ultimately use the cards, tarot readings and tarot spreads don't really work unless you're willing to listen to what the cards are communicating. If you're not in a space to hear any potential message from the cards, then a tarot reading probably isn't going to help your situation.

In general, don't ask the cards questions that you can't handle the answers to.

PART TWO

READING SPREADS

Tarot cards are pieces of stories, aspects of self, glimpses of truth. Each individual card has the power to offer us a window into ourselves, our communities, our challenges, our relationships, our dreams, and our potential. And every time we pull a tarot card for ourselves, every time we spend a few moments with the deck and let it offer us magic and truth, we deepen our relationship with the deck just a little bit more.

Although becoming fluent in the language of tarot can take time—even a lifetime—to master, your individual tarot readings do not have to be complicated. Anytime we grab our deck, focus our mind, and pull a card, we are deepening our tarot practice and strengthening our relationship with the cards. Even single-card pulls or quick morning meditations can do a lot to expand our perspective on the tarot, ourselves, and spirituality. While the tarot can rock our world with major insights or shake up our perspectives in truly transformative ways, every single tarot reading doesn't have to involve a cataclysmic personal shift. Sometimes we just need a quick check-in or bit of support.

There are countless ways to work with tarot cards. From readings to inspiration, from creative mapping to psychic journeys, from connecting with others to connecting with ourselves, the tarot truly is a tool with a wide range of uses, applications, and possibilities. And with seventy-eight different cards in the deck, the combinations of various cards number in the thousands, which is why reading with multiple cards at once can be both exhilarating and overwhelming.

For many who read tarot, spreads can offer a lot of power, clarity, and purpose to readings. Tarot spreads, intentional arrangements for tarot cards that include a particular meaning or prompt for each card, help us to ask focused, direct questions of our cards. They allow us to come at a situation from a variety of angles, honing in on specific aspects of our concern, or leaving space for the cards to fill in the gaps on their own. They also help us keep our particular question in mind, rather than wondering what exactly the cards are talking about. But if we're using a spread that is complicated, vague, or not the right layout for our question, sometimes a tarot spread can create more confusion than we started with.

When we use tarot spreads, we allow for more complexity, more layers, and more depth. And in this part of the book, we'll be tackling what it means to read a tarot spread, techniques for effective readings, and common questions that readers have when learning to read with spreads. You'll also find exercises so that you can practice reading tarot spreads for yourself.

What Are Tarot Spreads?

Tarot spreads are organized, structured layouts that organize our tarot readings. With a tarot spread, each card drawn is in response to a specific prompt, with each position working together in harmony to provide clear information, insights, wisdom, advice, or encouragement. Tarot spreads come in every size, from two-card spreads to ten-card spreads to spreads that use every single one of the deck's seventy-eight cards.

While new tarot spreads are written every day, there are also many classic spreads that have been used for decades by tarot practitioners. Three-card layouts like *past / present / future*, *mind / body / spirit*, and *situation / obstacle / advice* can be used for nearly any situation or question, and are often recommended for beginners who want to practice with a simple spread fairly early in their practice. By pulling one tarot card for each prompt, we immediately have a framework for the reading and context for each card that we're working with.

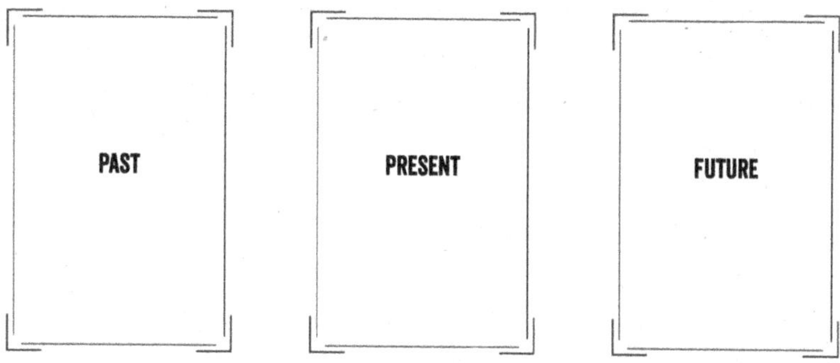

Regardless of their length, I like to think of tarot spreads as blueprints—a way of designing or mapping out what you want your tarot reading to cover. This intentional planning session occurs before any actual creation or building occurs, a period of drafting and deciding what will happen next.

Spreads let us dig into the structure of our reading, deciding in advance what we want to examine or consider with the cards. They allow us to be precise in our questions, clarify ahead of time what we hope to receive, and set our expectations for what the reading will explore. The process of spelling out exactly what we want to know, really drilling down about what we are bringing to the cards and hoping to receive in return, can often sharpen our queries and help us understand ourselves and our questions better too.

In other words, tarot spreads can help us fully understand our true intentions, to be honest with ourselves and with our cards about what we want to discuss, examine, and understand.

Because tarot spreads vary so widely, there are many different styles and sizes available. Although some readers prefer shorter spreads and others want to pull a lot of cards for their readings, there's not a "perfect number of cards" for a spread. The number used entirely depends on the reader, the question, and their preferences. Using larger spreads won't necessarily give more clarity, just more information. And the more cards you pull, the more interpretation you will need to do in order to understand what the cards are telling you.

Of course, tarot spreads are not at all mandatory for tarot readings. Anytime you pull a card from your deck with intention and awareness, you are reading tarot. But tarot spreads can add clarity and shape to your readings and are particularly useful when you are bringing a particular question, concern, or decision to the tarot, especially if you want to approach a situation from multiple angles.

How Do Tarot Spreads Work?

Spreads essentially function as guides for the conversation. They aren't necessarily better or worse than a more open, generalized reading. They are simply a different tool for your readings and work toward a different purpose.

Tarot spreads work by offering structure for the reading, directing the conversation that you are having with your cards in a particular direction or toward a certain angle. Rather than a free-flowing, open-ended question, a spread can create opportunities for clarity, discovery, insight, advice, support, or any number of other offerings from the cards. Spreads provide specific positions for each card to speak to. One card is drawn for each position and serves as an answer or response to whatever that position's question or prompt is.

Remember my analogy from Part One, about viewing our relationship with tarot like a relationship with a friend and seeing readings as conversations? Think about the difference between reaching out to a friend to catch up or chat versus connecting with them specifically to talk through a problem, make a request, or ask for advice. The first kind of conversation could go in any direction, could get deep and intense or stay light and fun, could twist and turn through different topics or end up focusing on one specific thing. There's not necessarily a specific expectation or result; it's just a chance to touch base, listen, and be present with your friend. But the second kind of conversation is addressing a particular need, creating an opportunity for you to ask directly for what you want. When we reach out to a friend with a particular request, we enter that conversation knowing what we are looking to receive and may even have specific questions or methods of support that we want to cover during that talk. We might know that our friend has a completely different perspective than we will have and could offer important truths or a viewpoint that helps us see the situation through another lens. Or we might know that we trust this friend's advice and want them to help us make a decision, choose a course of action, or adjust our expectations.

In both conversations, we are leaning on our knowledge of our friend and considering our expectations for the conversation we want to have before we ever reach out. Both kinds of conversations, whether generally catching up or seeking specific support, can be nourishing, powerful, clarifying, encouraging, and generous. But if we go into the conversation knowing what we want from our friend and feel confident in asking for it, we're far more likely to have the conversation that we want and to walk away with what we need.

Tarot spreads offer the same kind of choice. General readings leave room for anything, whether we're pulling a single card or many. These are readings like "What do I need to know today?" or "What should I be paying attention to right now?" or "What can you tell me about ____?" They leave space for the cards to go anywhere they like, to address whatever the tarot wants to address. But with spreads, we can make more detailed, specific asks. We can create an outline for the conversation, introducing not only the topic but the needs we have around that topic.

Why Do We Use Tarot Spreads?

While the cards can offer clarity in a variety of ways, tarot spreads can help us be more direct about what we want to know, explore, question, and understand. No matter our question, concern, or situation, tarot spreads empower us to be clear about what we need from our reading.

Here's an example: Consider that you have a question about your current job. You're feeling discouraged at work, having been passed over for a promotion that you felt you deserved, and are wondering if you should stay in your current position or start looking for opportunities elsewhere. Certainly, you could pull a card or two as a general reading and ask the tarot: "What do I need to know about my current job?" This kind of simple reading might give you just the kind of feedback you're looking for. You might get cards that perfectly capture those feelings of frustration, uncertainty, and lack of direction; that make you feel less alone; that help to validate your complicated emotions and honor where you are. However, you might also get cards that skew more into advice, that encourage you to stick it out and be patient, or that urge you to listen to your heart and start looking into making a career change. All of these are completely valid responses to your question and could be all the support you need.

With a tarot spread, on the other hand, you can get a lot more nuanced, a lot more granular, a lot more intentional, and ultimately receive more clarity and insight. You could do a two-card spread to help you make a decision about what to do, pulling one card for "stay" and one for "go," and see what comes up for each possibility.

You could do a three-card spread with positions for something you need to know about your current job, a new opportunity you might want to consider, and advice for how to move forward or what to do next. You could do a larger spread, with five or seven cards, exploring how you feel emotionally about this current position, what might be good about staying where you are, advice on how to talk to your manager, insights into taking care of yourself, something tangible you can do to make progress in your career, or any number of other angles. You could even do a ten-card Celtic Cross and see what the cards might reveal about your past, present, future, struggles, dreams, and possible outcomes. Any of these would be completely valid choices.

Pulling a single tarot card in this particular situation *might* give you what you need. But with a larger tarot spread, you can ask the cards for wisdom on different angles and outcomes, different possibilities and opportunities, and turn the reading into a much larger and more in-depth experience. If you're looking to be more precise in your readings around a particular situation, or if you want to lower the risk that you won't understand exactly what your deck is trying to tell you, a spread with multiple cards might be more useful for you.

The other reason to use tarot spreads is that by going through the process of selecting, writing, or revising a tarot spread for our reading, we can find a supported way to crystalize what it is we're looking for. Sometimes I will look at a bunch of spreads on a particular topic almost like suggestions: reading many different angles on a particular topic or challenge, paying attention to the prompts and questions I'm drawn to, and noting what resonates. Even if I don't use any of those spreads or ultimately decide not to work with a spread at all, the process of researching those spreads can help me find the exact language that I want to use for my own readings.

In short, we use tarot spreads to help dig deeper into a particular situation, question, topic, theme, or idea, and to give us more opportunities to receive the information, encouragement, support, advice, or clarity that we're seeking.

When Do We Use Tarot Spreads? When Do We *Not* Use Tarot Spreads?

Tarot spreads are the most useful when we have a clear idea of what we want from the tarot cards and when we have taken time to recognize how the cards can realistically help us out.

For complex questions, sticky situations, ongoing challenges, hard decisions, or any moment when you'd like more depth and breadth, when you're looking for something specific and *know* that tarot is the right tool for the job, a tarot spread can support a more rich and nuanced conversation with your cards. And the process of selecting, editing, and using a tarot spread can offer as much clarity as the reading itself if we're open to the journey.

It's just as important to know when to *not* use a spread as it is to know when one might be beneficial. Not every situation requires a tarot spread. In fact, I would argue that spreads are never *completely* necessary for clear and valuable tarot readings, especially since in some situations the wrong spread might make a reading more complicated or frustrating than it needs to be. It's important to recognize when a spread will be helpful and when it might do more harm than good.

If your question isn't particularly clear, or if you aren't sure what you actually want from the cards, a tarot spread that takes the conversation in a particular direction might end up leaving you lost, struggling, or even irritated. In this case, an open-ended reading might be more useful for you or help you clarify what your question is about.

If you find yourself nervous about receiving a particular card or answer, a spread might feel like a lot to tackle. At times when you're fearing a specific outcome or chanting to yourself "anything but *X* card!" I gently invite you to put down the deck and do something else: go for a walk, grab your journal, call a friend, drink some water, or participate in another activity that will calm your nervous system or support your emotions. Sometimes pulling a card when you aren't prepared for the cards to speak can add more stress than we need, so wait to work with the tarot until you're open to *any* card coming forward.

Reading with a tarot spread isn't a guarantee of clarity, but it can really help to focus your reading. However, choosing the right spread makes all the difference. If you're using a spread that doesn't address what you actually hope to receive, you may leave the reading with more questions than you started with. This experience can be particularly frustrating because the cards may offer things you don't need or want, pull you in a direction you don't want to go, or say things you aren't prepared to hear. It's important not to simply use the first spread on a particular topic that you find, but instead to take your time and make sure that the spread you're using will actually address your needs. (And to find a different spread, tweak an existing one, or write a completely new one if necessary, which we'll tackle later in the book.)

If you aren't sure what you're looking for or are being activated by fear, a spread might not be right for this particular reading. But if you know that a situation could benefit from some nuance, multiple questions, or ways to come at a problem from a variety of angles, a tarot spread can be an excellent tool for your reading.

Where Do Tarot Spreads Come From?

Using spreads to help guide or structure tarot readings is nothing new. The earliest published tarot spread on record is contained in Court de Gébelin's *Le Monde Primitif,* published in 1781. Of course, this in no way indicates that this is actually the first ever use of tarot spreads, or that this is the first tarot spread ever created. It's simply the earliest record that I've been able to find of a tarot spread being included in a published work. The Romani people were already offering card divination services using playing cards and other tools when the tarot was developed, but because their history relies more heavily on oral traditions than written ones, it's much harder to know if spreads have been used alongside tarot since the very beginning or if they developed along the way—or if the structures used for readings at that time have much in common with the tarot spreads that we use today.

Regardless of their origin, modern tarot spreads can come from many sources. From classic tarot spreads that have been used for a long time to brand new tarot spreads that are written and shared every day, there are hundreds, thousands, even potentially millions of tarot spreads that already exist in the world. Books boasting thousands of tarot spreads already exist, and most tarot books and deck guidebooks include spreads for readers to use. For some readers, tarot readings always utilize spreads, so having a wide variety available may feel essential.

Many tarot spreads have become classics for a reason. The ten-card Celtic Cross is one that is often recommended to readers of all ages and skill levels, for nearly any situation, because of its universal approach. (I personally do not recommend such a large spread for beginners, based on my own experiences, but you do you!) There are also a number of classic general three-card spreads that appear in nearly every tarot book published, like *mind / body / soul, past / present / future,* or *situation / obstacle / advice.* These kinds of spreads are great to keep in your back pocket, providing a baseline of structure while still leaving room for many questions or challenges to be addressed.

There is a lot of value in these kinds of tarot spreads because it means that we don't necessarily have to go hunting for a deeply precise, personalized spread just to do a tarot reading. But there will also be moments when you may crave more specificity, when you want to get more granular or detailed in the reading. Knowing when to use a more general spread and when to use a carefully curated, edited, or fully new spread is a matter of preference . . . and practice.

How Do We Choose a Particular Tarot Spread?

There are many different ways to choose a tarot spread, and the path you end up on entirely depends on where you begin. Choosing a spread can be a time-consuming process, especially if you're looking for something specific.

Sometimes, you may simply see a spread out in the world that you want to use, and decide to grab your deck and do a reading using it. From silly or casual spreads to more in-depth and intensive layouts, tarot spreads are written, shared, and published every day, in books, on blogs, and through social media. Some days, it's as easy as discovering a new tarot spread and feeling as though working with it on your own might offer something that you need in that particular moment.

Other times, we realize that we want to use a spread for a reading about a particular topic and therefore must go hunting for the one that suits us best. Many tarot books serve as encyclopedias and references for a wide variety of tarot layouts that you can use at your leisure. If you know that you want to use your cards to explore a particular topic, these kinds of resources are invaluable, as you can browse them quickly and easily, looking for one that aligns with your preferences.

Still other times, we may know that we want a spread that uses a specific position, method, or outcome. We might have a very clear idea of the kind of spread that would be helpful to us and end up searching for one that suits our vision. For this particular case, knowing how to edit or tweak existing spreads (or how to write your own spread from scratch) can be a very helpful skill.

Just like when doing a more open-ended reading without a spread, setting your intention for the reading is still important here. What do you hope to receive from this reading? What is your specific question? It can be tempting when using a tarot spread to not actually clarify your intention, but a spread is just a tool to help you make your intention even more clear, not a substitute for the intention altogether. What are you using the spread to help you accomplish, understand, clarify, explore, question, or decide? How is the spread offering definition to the reading you want to do and helping to ensure that your intention is met?

What Should We Look for in a Tarot Spread?

All spreads are different, and all spread writers are unique. But when you know how to read the general vibe and intention of a spread and can compare that spread's function with your own personal needs for a reading, it can help you find a layout that will help to facilitate the kind of conversation that you want to have with your cards. When you're assessing a tarot spread, it's essential to take note of the kinds of prompts that are included. Are they mainly introspective, action-oriented, or something else? Is the spread creating space for you to have a new perspective on something, to identify a feeling or desire, to make a decision, to challenge an idea, to gain advice? What possibilities are the positions inviting in? What pathways are they laying for you to follow?

Returning to our earlier example, a career spread that focuses entirely on how you feel about your current job might be great in some circumstances. However, if you specifically are looking for help from the tarot around deciding whether or not to start looking for a new job, and the spread you've selected doesn't include any positions or questions that provide advice, it will likely not end up giving you the kinds of answers you're craving.

To help get ahead of this frustration, I tend to think of spreads as falling into three distinct categories, depending on what they are exploring, what functions they serve, and why we might use them over another spread. (This is just my personal method; you might find it helpful to break these categories into smaller subgroups or may categorize spreads in a completely different way.) As mentioned earlier, taking the time to consider what exactly you're hoping to gain from your reading will help you assess your chosen spread with a critical and honest eye.

Are you looking for a spread that is introspective, one that asks clarifying questions and encourages you to look within? Are you trying to sort out something within yourself, to identify a feeling or need or fear, to work through something or come to a particular conclusion? Could you use an alternative viewpoint or more expansive perspective on something? Are you longing for *insight*?

Or are you looking for something tangible, an action item or set of steps that you can take to accomplish a particular goal? Are you craving direction, looking for a clear path forward? Are you wanting the cards to help provide you with something you can do immediately, offering clear and sound *advice*?

Or perhaps, are you aware of what is happening and know what you need to do, but are hoping to find some encouragement, compassion, or care from the cards to follow through or take action? Are you looking for reminders of why this is important, what you are working toward, how your needs might be met along the way? Are you eager for *support*?

Some spreads fit neatly into one category, while others simultaneously make space for more than one of these themes! Identifying which of these needs you're hoping to fill—whether it's one, two, or all three desires—can help you look at possible spreads more critically and take into consideration how the card positions in the spread will tangibly address your concerns. Particularly when you're choosing between several spreads, this approach can help you narrow down your decision and select a spread that will effectively structure your reading.

An easy way to tell what the spread will leave you with is to look not only at all of the positions included in the layout, but specifically to consider the final card. If that last card in the spread makes space for a tangible action you could take, like "something to try" or "a next step," this is likely an advice-focused spread. If the last card is more insight-focused, it may end with a card like "something to be aware of" or "a truth to sit with." And spreads that end with cards like "a strength you hold" or "a gift to remember" are likely support-focused spreads.

Another thing to keep in mind when choosing a layout is the spread's length, or the number of cards in the spread. I've said it before and I'll say it again: Spreads don't have to be long to be effective, and shorter readings can often be easier to understand and engage with. More cards can mean more potential for confusion, whereas fewer positions mean there is less room for murky answers or uncertainty. I personally prefer tarot spreads that use between two and five cards, but I've been known to do much larger readings when the time calls for it, or if it feels as though every position truly adds something unique to the conversation. There's certainly nothing wrong with longer spreads, and if you love long readings, that's wonderful! But don't mistake many card positions for many insights. More cards is not always better; it really depends on your question, your capacity, your experience, and your preferences. Some of the most powerful readings I've given and received used only a few cards!

When trying to choose a spread, pay attention to each position, and consider what it contributes to the overall purpose of the reading. How does each card offer something different to the topic or theme? What does it add to the conversation? How does it provide something new or distinct from the other cards in the layout? And is this length of reading something that you feel comfortable navigating?

Sometimes spreads that use a lot of cards can be repetitive, while other times it's very clear how each card contributes to the overall narrative and flow of the spread. Be discerning, and make sure that you're using a spread that will actually address your question—without a lot of filler. Too many cards, in positions that are too similar, and you may end up with more questions than answers by the end of the reading.

What If My Question Is Really Complicated?

There is a big difference between asking the cards about a complicated *situation* and having a question that *itself* is complicated. Many situations are complicated and include difficult history, challenges and struggles, hard decisions, and tangled emotions. The tarot can hold space for incredibly hard moments and can help us to parse our own feelings, help us make choices, and show us different ways to navigate these struggles.

Yet being in the midst of a complicated situation does not necessarily mean that *the question itself* is going to be complicated.

Here's an example: Say you have a friend who has been with one romantic partner for a long time. They've been through thick and thin together, have navigated challenges and celebrated victories. Yet your friend is struggling with whether or not they are really compatible as a couple, in light of a lengthy rough patch in the relationship. In communicating with your friend, they might want to talk through a lot of nuance with you, looking at the pros and cons of the relationship, honoring their feelings and desires, getting very specific about all of the many obstacles they have worked through and the ones that still remain. But when it's time to pull cards, the questions themselves might be incredibly simple: Is this relationship one that your friend wants to remain in? Or is it perhaps time to end the relationship for good?

Answering these questions could be as simple as a three-card general reading and could use a general spread like the *problem / solution / advice*. This spread includes a card for the problem, bringing attention to the current challenge that your friend is facing in the relationship. The second card offers a clear and simple solution to this problem, as the tarot has defined it. And the final card provides some advice on how to implement this solution, with a tangible path forward.

This same situation also could be explored with the Celtic Cross, a ten-card spread that includes positions for self or present, the current problem, the past, the future, what's conscious, what's unconscious, your friend's influence, an external influence, hopes and fears, and a potential outcome. This is still a general spread, but its positions create space for many more aspects of the situation, allowing for a deeper dive into your friend's present emotions, what the current problem in the relationship is, past issues that may be impacting the present, where things may go if nothing is changed, something your friend already knows, something they haven't fully recognized or acknowledged, what your friend can control in the situation, an outside influence that is impacting things, your friend's hopes and fears for the relationship, and a potential outcome that summarizes the entire reading.

However, your friend might want to get more specific or have more personal questions about this relationship. They may be worried about an aspect of their past, be angry about something that is currently disrupting the relationship, have a deep fear or desire around staying together or breaking up, or feel strongly that they don't want any kind of outcome position included in the reading. In this case, writing a customized spread might be a better option, to allow for a more personalized reading that addresses their specific concerns.

What's fascinating about tarot reading, and choosing a spread, is that, in all likelihood, the results of the reading, regardless of which of these spreads is used, will be the same! But the path to getting there and the facets of the situation that are included and explored in the reading may be very different—and in an emotional situation like this example, a spread that includes positions of care or that approaches the situation with gentleness and compassion could make all the difference in how your friend feels when the reading is over. When you know what the querent needs to feel safe, heard, and supported, you can customize a spread to ensure that they leave the reading in the best possible mindset, even if the cards themselves are challenging.

What I'm saying is that a well-crafted tarot spread, regardless of its length or specificity, can deliver a very accurate, powerful, and useful reading, no matter the complexity of the situation or question. It's all about learning how to work with the structure that the spread provides, and understanding the relationship between the cards, the positions, and the overall flow of the reading.

How Are Tarot Spreads Presented?

Many tarot spreads are shared as graphics, with clear positions for each card. These are often the most beginner-friendly, as the position is connected directly to each card, and you can choose to lay your cards out on your reading surface in the same order and shape that appears in the graphic. (But remember, you absolutely don't have to! You can lay the cards out in any shape or order you like—just make sure to pay attention to how you're doing it, so that you don't get confused.) In such a case, the card positions are numbered, and the question or prompt corresponds to the numbered position of the card. Other times, the prompt may be written directly onto the image, corresponding to each card outline.

However, you may also see tarot spreads written out as text-only prompts, or that primarily use alt text on images. You may find it helpful to visualize these spreads in a similar way, or you may find that you prefer text-only spreads, especially if you like pulling more than one card for each position.

A text-only spread might be written out like so: *you / your partner / what to keep / what to let go / next step.* Just like with the graphics, you'll pull one card for each prompt. Many of the spread suggestion prompts in this book will be written out in this way, and you hereby have my express permission to arrange the cards in whatever shape you like and pull them in a different order if you prefer.

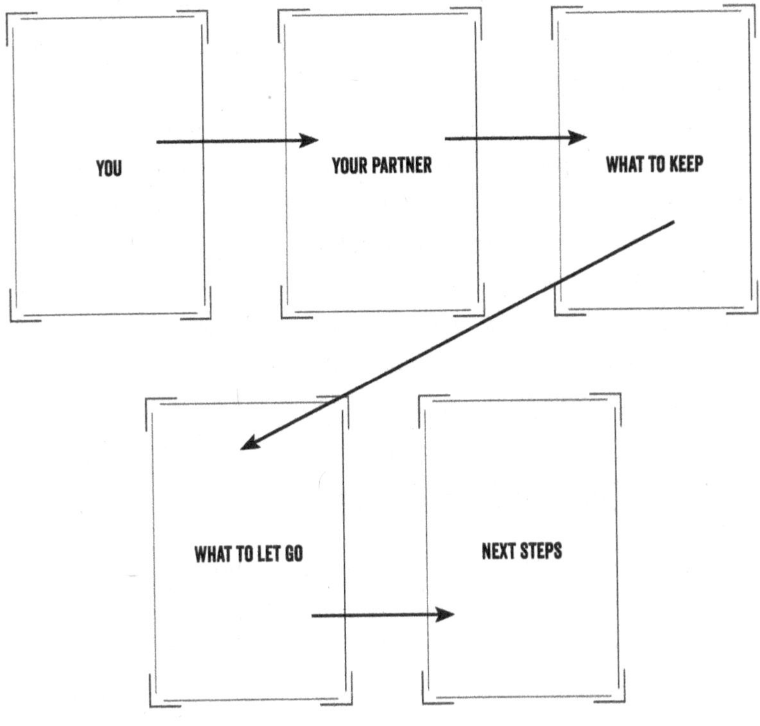

Most tarot spreads will have you pull one card for each prompt or position, as reflected in the graphics and written-out example spreads shared here. I personally tend to read spreads from left to right, pulling cards in the order in which they appear in that direction, but this is only one method for pulling cards. You may prefer to move from right to left, top to bottom, bottom to top, or to follow another sequence. Some spreads might call for the cards to be arranged in a particular shape, like a circle or square, or a more elaborate pattern, in which case you can decide for yourself which order you want to pull the cards in. Other spreads may indicate for you to lay a card on top of another card in a cross pattern.

Whether or not you actually physically lay the cards out in the exact position called for by a tarot spread graphic is entirely up to you. The spread will still "work" even if you lay the cards out in a straight line. However, whichever order you pull your cards in, make sure that you are noting which card you are drawing for each position so that you don't get mixed up about which card is answering each question. If you aren't interested in (or don't have the space for) laying out the cards to mirror the graphic, you may find it helpful to redesign the spread before pulling cards, or to write down the card positions on scraps of paper and lay them on top of or beside the cards you draw so that you can keep your reading straight. It can be really frustrating to pull a series of cards only to lose track of which card goes in each position!

A Note on Outcomes and Predictions

I spoke on this topic briefly in the first part of this book, but particularly when it comes to choosing and using a tarot spread, it's *essential* to be clear about your beliefs for tarot readings. Whether you use tarot predictively or not, knowing what you expect from the cards and how you process those answers will make a big difference in the ways that you read and the meanings that you make from the cards that come forward.

What do I mean by *reading predictively*? Most tarot readings can be considered divination in a broad sense, as divination is related generally to discovering hidden knowledge through the use of occult or mystical tools. But when we read tarot predictively, we are actively working to predict or foretell the future. In other words, we are asking the cards what *will* happen. Divination has a long and robust history in various cultures throughout history and is an extremely legitimate and popular way to use the tarot (and other divination tools).

While I believe that tarot as a tool can be used for basically anything, depending on the practitioner, I personally do not read tarot with the main objective of predictions, a preference that is reflected not only in my personal readings but also in my client work, the spreads that I write for individuals, as well as my more general offerings to the public. I mention this because my own tarot spreads tend to end with suggested next steps, something that can be done right now, or another suggestion that gives control to the person being read for, rather than a set destiny or "outcome" card. I personally believe that the tarot can advise us on what is likely to happen based on our current actions and choices, but that the future is not fixed and that we can choose our own path based on the information that the tarot offers. However, your own beliefs may be very different, and that is absolutely okay.

All of this is important to note because many tarot spreads, particularly in the final position or the last card of the layout, will have a prompt like "what will happen next" or "the outcome of this decision." Depending on how you choose to read and interpret that prompt, this can feel very definitive, pointing to a guaranteed outcome of a particular decision, observation, or action. But you can also choose to read these prompts as a potential outcome, as something that *may* happen rather than something that will *absolutely* happen. It's entirely up to you to decide, and both methods of interpretation can work very well. You just need to know which one you're doing in your own readings.

It's essential that you take the time to consider your tarot beliefs *before* you do a reading and end up with a card in a final predictive position that might really scare or upset you. Using tarot spreads that reflect your perspectives, or taking care to thoughtfully interpret any positions that may not align with your beliefs, is an important part of building a supportive and aligned personal tarot practice.

How Do We Read Tarot Spreads?

Reading tarot spreads is a foundational practice, one that you can use regardless of whether you're using a spread written by someone else or one that you've created on your own. This is an art form, a deepening relationship, and can take time to develop. Every tarot reading, especially when we're using a tarot spread, is an opportunity for discovery, expansion, insight, clarity, and magic. The *how* of reading tarot spreads is very personal, so we're going to approach this process through a few different lenses.

Before we dig in, I want to stress again that the most important thing to remember when using tarot spreads is to be *consistent*. Reading tarot is a practice, something that will grow and develop over time, that has the potential to change no matter how long you've been working with the cards. And the more that you use spreads, the more natural and easeful it will feel. But if you are just getting started reading spreads, or have been struggling to read spreads for a while and want to revisit the fundamentals, my advice remains the same: *be patient with yourself and with the process.* Utilizing spreads is not always easy, and some readings can be very challenging. Give yourself plenty of time to read, to reflect, to listen.

If you've been working with tarot for some time already, you may already have rituals around tarot readings that feel as natural as breathing. You may already always use the same process, the same shuffling style, the same approach to your cards. But if you're newer to tarot, it might take a bit of experimentation to develop a routine that feels good. Don't be afraid to try different shuffling styles, to see if you like always lighting a candle or sipping on the same kind of tea, to read in the same place or to mix it up. Play around, test techniques, and see what your natural preferences are.

If you are just getting started with a tarot practice, try some short general readings first to learn what feels good for you. Which decks feel good in your hands? What art speaks to you? Where do you like to sit or stand or pace around while reading? How do you enter your tarot reading space or mindset? What helps to keep you grounded and focused? Do you like music, something to drink, a blanket, a candle, or incense? Do you like to be alone, or do you read in community with someone else like a partner, roommate, friend, pet, or family member? Do you like to read in public or in private? Do you always shuffle the same number of times? Do you have a set method for choosing the cards that you'll read? Do you prefer to journal your way through a reading, or do you like to sit quietly? Is your tarot reading connected to your spiritual or religious practice?

It's okay if you don't have the answers to all of (or *any* of) these questions. They're not meant to overwhelm you. But for many people it can be helpful to have a baseline practice, no matter how simple, before tackling tarot spreads.

Personally, I don't have a specific spot in my house where I pull cards. I've read in my kitchen, my office, my living room, my dining room, even on the floor! I like to have tea by my side, but it's not a requirement. Same with a candle or incense—it's lovely but not necessary. I do like to take a few deep breaths to center myself and get my focus together, and if my mind is very restless or active, I work to quiet it. I have a variety of decks that I work with, but regardless of which card set I'm using, my process is the same: I shuffle the cards while thinking about my question or the topic that I want to tackle. If I'm using a tarot spread, I read through the positions while shuffling, asking for perception, focus, and clear messages. I continue to mix the cards until my mind has stilled. Then I split the deck into three piles, stack them onto one another, and lay my hands over the deck. I close my eyes, take a deep breath in, and let it out slowly. Then I draw cards from the top of the pile and lay them out on my reading surface from left to right.

If I'm using a tarot spread, I will read each position that I'm drawing for as I pull the card, flipping it over so that I can see which prompt the deck is responding to. Some people prefer to pull cards face down and flip them over only one at a time. I like to draw each card for each position one after another, face up, then begin the reading once the cards are fully laid out. If I'm not using a tarot spread, I'll simply look at the cards as a group and see what they have in common, paying attention to what ideas, themes, or messages come forward. But with a spread, there are usually more pointed messages, more clear ideas to work with.

Remember that when we use a tarot spread, we are establishing parameters for the conversation that we want to have with the cards. We are telling the tarot exactly what kinds of feedback, insights, encouragement, support, advice, and action items we want to receive, and we are creating a map or blueprint for how that conversation is going to flow.

Once you have the cards pulled, you can begin the process of *reading* them.

I like to start by looking at the group of cards as a whole. Does anything immediately jump out about the collection of cards in this reading? Are there any similarities in terms of suit, element, number, color, energy? Do the cards tell a clear story, even before referring back to the tarot spread? If there's a repeating number or suit, how might that give you an early indication of the vibe or energy of the reading?

Once noting overall themes, I then look at each card individually and consider what that card has to offer about the position it was pulled for. Imagine the card in a conversation with the prompt it's responding to. If the prompt is a question, how does the card answer that question? If the prompt is a challenge or an urge to reflect, how does that card offer a clarifying insight? If the prompt is a piece of advice or a next step, how does this card provide an example of something that can be done?

There's no need to rush this process. Take as much time as you like.

If it initially feels as though a card has nothing to do with its prompt, step back from the meanings and keywords you usually ascribe to the card and think instead about the energy of that card, what it's working toward or responding to. Just because this is an unexpected answer doesn't mean that it isn't still a response. How might this card be offering a new perspective on the situation, question, theme, topic, or challenge?

After I've gone through each individual card and considered what it might be saying about its particular position, I return to looking at the reading as a whole. I like to think about what each card is pointing me to next, and honor the flow and story that the cards are telling. How is each card offering a piece of the puzzle?

While each card is in conversation with the position it was pulled for, the cards are also all in conversation with one another. In looking at them side by side, and in considering which messages they are presenting on their own, we can start to see bigger, brighter messages reveal themselves. How does each card support the others' messages? Where are there contradictions?

If I'm struggling to understand even one card, or if I find myself confused by the overall message, this is the point when I journal about it. I often find that in trying to write about what I'm confused by, clarity emerges. But even if it doesn't, having a record of your initial reaction to the reading can be incredibly useful down the line, as sometimes the reading becomes more clear in the hours or days or even weeks to come.

Finally, after looking at individual cards, studying the reading as a whole, and journaling through any challenges as needed, I finish the reading by looking carefully at the final card of the spread. Whether I've written the spread myself or am using one from another creator, the last card in a tarot reading often serves as a next step, action item, or idea to carry forward into the rest of my day. What does that last card offer as something that I can consider, remember, respect, do, try, or release? How might that final message serve as an overall insight into the reading as a whole?

A well-written spread should have positions that not only offer a new perspective or piece of information but also set up the card that is to follow. If you get stuck on a particular card and can't figure out what it's trying to say, look at the card in the position before or after. How might that card offer some additional insight into the card you're stuck on?

What If I Get Stuck?

It's extremely, incredibly normal to get tripped up during tarot readings. Sometimes I think it's even more likely to happen when using a spread, simply because there's more information to manage; sometimes we may pull a card for a specific position and not understand the connection between the two. *This does not make you a bad tarot reader!* Being confused about a reading means you are one of us: because it happens all the time and is simply part of the process. Even the most experienced tarot readers sometimes pull a card and have no idea what it's trying to communicate.

If you get stuck, the first thing I will tell you to do is *breathe*. Tarot reading isn't a race, and there's no deadline for truth. Take a moment to recenter, calm your emotions, and breathe with intention. The cards aren't going anywhere.

The second thing is to resist the urge to berate yourself for not knowing enough. All the tarot knowledge and experience in the world don't necessarily prepare you for every possible reading. Show yourself compassion and gentleness, and remember that every single tarot reading expands your overall knowledge of this practice.

The third is to look closely at the card that's tripping you up and try to figure out what exactly is confusing for you. Is the card itself one that you struggle with regularly? Getting back to basics on the card's meaning and how you work with it might help, which could mean looking at key correspondences, exploring your own notes or past readings with this card, or checking out resources for additional perspectives.

Is the position that the card landed in vague, confusing, or unclear to you? Take a moment to tease out what the prompt is really getting at, either by rewriting it for yourself (take care not to change the meaning, only to clarify it!) or by journaling around what it could be exploring.

Do both the card and the position make sense separately but not together? This can be the trickiest challenge to navigate, but it's not unsolvable. First, try taking a step back and assessing the general energy and impact of the card itself. Does this card seem to be portraying conflict, stability, movement, stillness, choice, confusion, or something else? What is the card offering? Then, consider how that energy intersects with the position that the card is in. Is the position one that is seeking clarity, offering advice or perspective, pushing you to think about something in a new way? How might this card answer that call?

Here's an example: Say I'm doing a reading on a really tender relationship topic, and in a position called "how I feel about this person," I pull Temperance. Temperance is a card that trips up a lot of people because it has so many meanings, and so many of those meanings can feel really big and theoretical rather than practical: moderation, balance, patience, alchemy. What could this archetype possibly have to tell me about my emotions?

To start, I would consider how Temperance feels to me, in my body. When I think about Temperance, I experience a sense of calm, peace, confidence in who I am, the knowledge that I might not have all of the answers but that I'm in the position to find them. This position is one of emotion, so now that I've considered how the card itself makes me feel, I can take those meanings and apply them to the reading: I feel calm with this person, even if I don't feel completely in control. There might be some curiosity, some eagerness to discover more, but there might also be more confidence and certainty than I'd initially recognized. This reading might be wanting me to acknowledge that I'm not as confused about this person as I think—or at least, that my feelings for this person are not at the heart of the issue that I'm pulling cards around.

Getting stuck in a reading can be really frustrating, especially if you grabbed your cards hoping for clarity. But as much as possible, slow down, take your time, and give yourself room to explore.

No, but Really—What If the Whole Reading Doesn't Make Sense to Me? What If Most of the Cards Are Confusing and I Just Don't *Get* What I'm Seeing?

Walk away.

I'm serious. Leave the cards where they are and take a lap. Get some water, have a snack, go watch television, go for a run, whatever—but stop looking at the cards and stop thinking about them. Fully separate yourself from the reading. You might even prefer to take a photo of the cards and then put the deck away entirely so that you have the record without the reminder.

Sometimes, distance is the only thing that brings clarity. Sitting there obsessively poring over card interpretations and researching card combinations and freaking out about what something might mean almost never reveals the answers—but these actions are almost guaranteed to leave you even more stressed, anxious, or frustrated.

Take as much time as you can from the reading, and revisit it only when you feel like you can approach the cards with a clean slate. Even if you're just as confused as before, your emotions will likely be calmer and more even, and you may still find new truths or insights that help things click into place.

Resist the impulse to redo the reading in the hopes of pulling new cards. I find that redoing it rarely ends well, as my decks often get salty with me rather than offering new clarity. However, if on revisiting the reading you still feel confused and want to turn to the deck for answers, leave the spread out (or pull out the same cards, if you put the reading away) and then separate out the specific cards that felt confusing to you. Shuffle the rest of the deck and pull a clarifying card for each of the original cards that confused you. Remember that these are not additional cards for the reading; they're instead available to help you understand what the original card meant.

I don't generally recommend pulling clarifying cards on a regular basis, as I find that it can easily distort the original readings, which is why I haven't included this particular technique in earlier sections. I tend to consider clarifying cards a last resort, though your experience may be very different. From my perspective, it's easy to get caught up in the clarifying card's message, to take that as the "final answer" over the original card. Whether you regularly use clarifying cards or not, make sure you do so with clarity and intention.

Examples and Exercises

1. Practice readings using different spreads. Reading a spread is not the same as reading multiple cards together in a more general reading. And while we might use some of the same skills to do so, the following examples and exercises are meant to offer you a jumping-off point—some playful ways to explore weaving the stories of several cards together in a cohesive and useful way.

For our first example, let's look at a three-card reading.

Before you read my thoughts on these three cards, take a few moments to consider what this general three-card reading might have to say. What do the cards have in common? What story do they tell? How do they connect to one another, and where might they contradict one another? What do you think this reading is about? How would you read these cards if they came up for you in a general reading that you were doing for yourself or for a friend?

____

____

____

____

____

____

____

____

____

____

The following interpretation is just one example of a reading for these cards, and as with all tarot readings, it is simply one potential way to view these cards. If in your notes or musings you reached a different set of conclusions, that is absolutely fine! This is just meant to show you one way to understand this reading, not to make a definitive declaration about the only way to look at these cards together.

Without a spread, these cards still have a lot in common. Two cards from the suit of pentacles, plus a major arcana card that is often associated with abundance, generosity, and expression, feel like a reading that is about home, community, care, and self-love. The Ten of Pentacles begins with a steady, solid energy, inviting us into a reading with a rich foundation, flowing resources, plenty for everyone. The Empress offers us anything that we may need, creativity and flow, playful joy, tapping into the collective, creating space for connection and for rest. And the Queen of Pentacles reminds us of the value of boundaries, of moving at a pace that works for us, of tapping into the resources that are already at our disposal to build the kind of world that we dream about.

When we look at these cards together, there's a general energy of warmth, control, stability, power, and abundance: Pentacles as earth, Ten as the culmination of the cycle, the Queen offering rulership and guidance, the Empress providing sweetness and Venusian beauty. All in all, a gentle, affirming trio of cards that encourage us to find comfort in all that we have, accept the love that is already flowing all around us, and remember how supported and adored we are.

While this reading may have been done about any number of topics, as a general reading it feels like a call to slow down, celebrate what is good, honor the resources that are present and the ones that are growing, and take pride in the work we have done to get to this point.

General readings are wonderful for assessment, a check-in, or reflection on a particular topic. But if we look at these three cards through the sharper lens of a spread, we can find something more. A spread would give this reading additional context and may help us refine our interpretation of each card in a more specific or pointed way.

Let's look at these same cards, in this same order, now through the perspective of a three-card spread.

SITUATION **OBSTACLE** **ADVICE**

These cards, which already told a specific story, now are answering more specific questions, pointing to particular challenges and offering ways to move through those challenges. This is a fairly simple and popular advice spread, but it has plenty to offer us in terms of what is going on and what we might do about it.

As you did with the general reading, take a few moments before you continue reading to practice plugging these three cards into this three-card spread. How does each card respond to the prompt that it was drawn for? In looking at each card through a specific lens, how does its meaning shift or clarify? What story do these cards now tell? How does your reading of this spread differ from looking at these cards through a more general viewpoint?

____

____

____

____

____

____

___

___

___

Again, the following is simply one potential interpretation of this spread! Do not worry if your own reading of this spread is different from mine. Instead, consider what you noticed and how these cards have spoken to you specifically. What do these cards have to say to you?

The Ten of Pentacles as a situation takes on a new meaning: There is stability here, but perhaps something has gone as far as it can go in a particular direction. Tens are fulfillment, a suit being pushed as far as it can go, but Ten is also the end of the cycle, making way for a new one. This card holds a lot of potential. The stability that is present for this querent may be solid right now, but something new may be beginning soon, something that might cause some of this energy to shift. As a present situation, this card may indicate that there's some anxiety or uncertainty about how long this abundance will last or what it might mean for it to change.

The second card, the Empress, is now in the position of the obstacle. And it's always very interesting when cards that we associate with "positive" ideas like joy, abundance, and creativity are in positions that explore complexity, challenges, obstacles, or something difficult. What does it mean for the Empress to be an obstacle? What first comes to mind is that there is a deep desire for expression, community, support, love, abundance, generosity, but that this is tripping the querent up somehow, getting in the way. Perhaps there's a notion that this longing for joyful outpouring, for playful exploration, for expression without perfection, could disrupt the stability that is already present in the Ten of Pentacles. Whether real or imagined, the Empress's loving connection, ability to hold space, and longing for authentic emotion are getting in the way of movement for this person. This person may feel that they cannot access the Empress's energy. Or it may be that the longing for visibility is causing challenges in relationships, work/life balance, or resource management. It could even be that there's some impatience for celebration, a desire to be praised for what we've done that isn't happening quickly enough.

Our final card, the Queen of Pentacles, is advice. And mirroring the same suit as the first card in this reading, the Queen shows a shift from moving cycles to a more stable, grounded energy. Queens are leaders, teachers, guides, experts of their element, and artists who know how to wield their element to its full capacity. As advice, this feels like a call to take ownership of what is going on, ground into self, and take comfort in the things that we can control. The Queen of Pentacles doesn't make things more complicated than they need to be and has a good relationship with boundaries. They know the value of work and play and rest, of connection and solitude, of using what is needed and sharing whenever possible. As advice, this feels like a suggestion to slow down, care for the self, and celebrate the stability and resources that we already have access to, bringing others into our abundance as we can.

Overall, this spread shifts the meaning of the reading in a new direction. Rather than simply feeling like a celebration of stability and resources, now we see a story of someone who might be afraid to trust that the abundance they are experiencing will last or is craving a sense of security that they cannot seem to find, yet is being called to slow down, trust that what they are doing is having the desired effect, and continue to invest in things that can actually be controlled. Whereas the general reading felt like an affirmation of everything being solid, steady, and supported, the spread introduces some deeper dives into potential internal struggles and offers some insights into how to address those personal challenges.

How might this three-card reading shift if we use a completely different tarot spread? How does the message change?

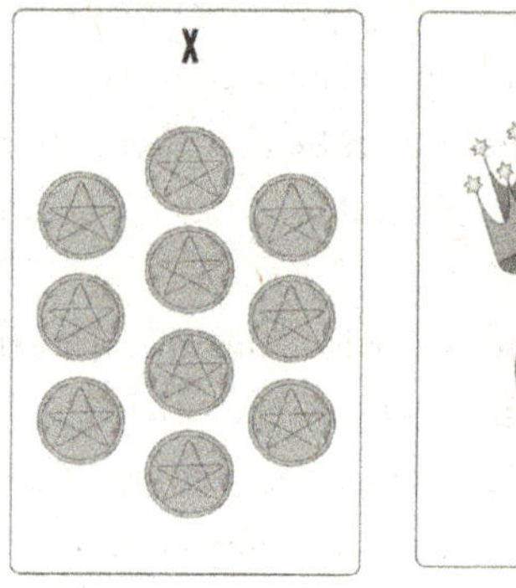

RED LIGHT **YELLOW LIGHT** **GREEN LIGHT**

One final time, take a few moments to read these cards through the lens of this spread. While this is a less common general spread, it's still one that is useful in a number of applications. *Red light* refers to something that should stop, either permanently or temporarily. *Yellow light* refers to something that should slow down, pause, or proceed with caution. And *green light* is all systems go, a call to keep moving forward at a safe but consistent pace. How would you read these cards in this spread? How do their meanings change? What does each of these cards have to offer?

____

____

____

____

____

____

Remember that the following is just one potential reading of this spread, and it's absolutely okay if your tarot reading is different from mine!

While the Ten of Pentacles is a card that speaks to stability, groundedness, and being well-resourced, the position of red light shifts the ways that we might read this card. Why would we want to *stop* feeling secure and resourced? This is where our reading skills come in. Tens are the culmination of a suit, pushing the energy or element to its absolute limit, a liminal energy of ending one journey and starting to anticipate the next. And the suit of pentacles, the element of earth, refers to the physical: our bodies, our money, our homes, our sense of safety and responsibility, the resources that we lean on, the ways that we protect ourselves. As a red light, this card takes on a new meaning and may speak to ways that we are being too cautious, too protective, too risk-averse. Perhaps we've been too focused on setting boundaries, shielding ourselves, or getting to a particular finish line, but now is the time to pause on that goal, to shift our focus. We've done as much as we can do in that arena, and it's time to move our energy into a new goal. Or we've become so obsessed with security that we're not letting in other joys, pleasures, or freedoms, and it's beginning to get in the way of other important aspects of our lives like relationships, adventure, or creative exploration.

The Empress, in the position of yellow light, also takes on a new meaning. Creativity, abundance, and collective care are beautiful things. Why would we want to slow down these flows? Yet if we have been spending too much of our energy and attention on caring for others, or are so focused on abundance that we're not investing in anything else, this might be a call to step back and carefully assess how we've been working, playing, and collaborating. Are we giving too much of ourselves away? Have we been generous to the point that we're being taken advantage of? Or perhaps, are we so focused on caring for ourselves that we need to look outward and attend to a partner or friend who could use our support?

Finally, our green light card: the Queen of Pentacles. I read Queens as community leaders who are in control of their work and play, who understand the necessity of boundaries and know how to extend compassion to those around them. And in this position, the Queen of Pentacles feels like an urging to get organized and simplify. Particularly in light of the other two cards, which may indicate a lot of hard work and attention to output, this Queen may be urging us to delegate some of those many tasks, show ourselves some care, and recognize what is most important. What deserves our focus and attention, and what can we set to the side for a time?

In going through this exercise, you can see how even though the cards themselves don't change, our interpretation of the cards can. Paying close attention to the position that the card is in can indicate which aspect of the card's meaning to explore, focus on, or even question.

Did any of the reading positions feel especially accessible to you? Did any of them feel particularly challenging to read? Take some time to reflect on your favorites.

• • •

2. Read with friends. Reading tarot can be a really intimate experience, and for a lot of people, serious or complicated spreads are things that you might want to tackle on your own. There's no shame in that. However, if you're comfortable, another practice exercise that I highly recommend is to read tarot spreads with other people. Reading with a partner or a group is a really fantastic way to get more comfortable working with tarot spreads. Even if no one in the group feels super confident or is highly experienced with reading spreads, going through the process of reading alongside other people and sharing your thoughts, ideas, questions, and confusions can be helpful, motivating, and also bring some lightheartedness into your readings.

If you have a small group of trusted friends, or even just a single person that you feel comfortable reading a more intensive or personal spread with, the sky is really the limit. You can definitely try a longer or more personal spread and tackle a serious challenge or a major concern that you might have alongside another person if you're concerned that you won't be able to be clear-eyed enough to read objectively.

However, if you want to practice reading tarot spreads more regularly, or if you're struggling to get better at spreads in general and you don't necessarily want to *also* have to do a lot of intensive emotional investigation at the same time, I recommend perhaps trying a spread that's a little bit more playful and reading it with a group. The last part of this book is packed with different spreads for many occasions, but here you can find a handful of spreads that I particularly like for reading with a group or a partner. These are fairly general but fun spreads that you can use that will help you learn how to get more comfortable reading spreads, but won't necessarily push you to a really intensive place that requires a lot of emotional vulnerability with other people.

something that connects us / something that we all love / something for us to explore together

something old / something new / something challenging / something comforting

a gift / a question / an open door

yesterday / today / tomorrow

• • •

3. Practice tricky cards. For our final exercise in this section, let's look at an example of a simple three-card spread that has some challenging cards in it. I want you to practice reading cards that might be more complicated or unexpected in particular positions. Practicing a difficult reading like this, especially when it's not a reading specifically for you, can be a little bit easier than learning on the fly and struggling with a reading that feels emotionally volatile. Even if you skip some of the other exercises, I highly recommend at least *attempting* this one, as pretty much every tarot reader I've ever known has done a reading that left them scratching their head.

For this example, we're going to return to our old friend: *situation / obstacle / advice*. This general three-card spread can be used for nearly any situation, which makes it a great basic layout for challenges, decisions, and, in our case, practice readings.

Let's say that we want to do a tarot reading around going to a particular event for the holidays. The holidays can be really fraught, and sometimes we receive an invitation to a certain place that might not feel safe, comfortable, or welcoming. Or we just might straight up not want to go, due to energy, time, finances, or lack of interest. But social pressure is a real thing, and sometimes it's easier to say yes to something than it is to say no! Perhaps in this example, a family member that we don't particularly get along with invited us to their annual holiday bash, and we had an awful time last year. We know that other family members might feel some kind of way if we skip it, but we also know that it will likely be a stressful event rather than a fun or relaxing one. Do we go to the party or not? We grab our tarot deck and pull three cards:

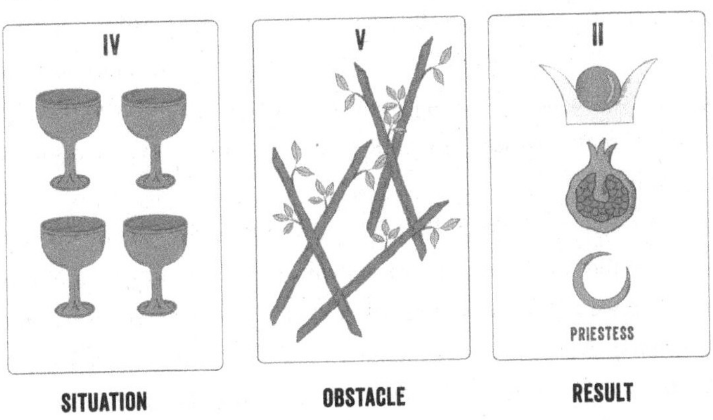

Before I offer my own interpretation, take some time to look at this reading and to imagine that you pulled these cards for yourself or for a loved one. How would you interpret this reading? Do any of the cards confuse you or leave you scratching your head?

The first two cards in this reading might seem fairly clear. The situation being represented as the Four of Cups speaks to a desire for emotional boundaries and perhaps a deep longing to remain separate from a group of people that we don't necessarily feel comfortable with or even welcome around. The Four of Cups can be a sticky card because sometimes it's defined as selfishness or emotional withholding. Yet in this position, the Four of Cups feels as though it represents a desire to protect our hearts and to not put ourselves in a position of vulnerability for no real reason other than pride or not wanting to rock the boat with our family.

Similarly, the Five of Wands in the position of an obstacle represents conflict. Fives are the messy middle or a pivot point, and with the suit of wands we tend to think first about interpersonal conflict—fights that don't really have a victor, or feelings of a restless lack of direction. In this position as the obstacle, this card can really represent a sensation of friction without purpose, frustration without an outlet. Going to this party might upset us without really accomplishing anything, and we're wrestling through this conflict that feels as though it doesn't have any good outcomes.

The final card for advice is the Priestess, which often represents observation, patience, inner wisdom, and contemplation. This is an archetype of balance, duality, and partnership, among other things. In this position, the Priestess might feel really frustrating to see because it seems to be saying that we should just trust our gut and do what we want. However, this is a tarot reading. Aren't we pulling cards because we *don't* know what we want? How can we trust our gut if we don't know what our gut is saying? How can we be calm when all we feel is fiery anxiety and irritation for being put in this position?

Personally, I would read the Priestess in this position as permission to skip the party. To me, the fact that cards are being pulled around this issue, and the fact that the other two cards are cards of challenge and frustration and uncertainty, wanting to protect the self, wanting to maybe not necessarily get into fights that aren't gonna go anywhere, all really speaks to a desire for calm and a need for space, as well as a longing to do what is best for us and prioritize our own authentic desires. Just like all Two cards, the Priestess often really speaks to a choice, yet it feels as though there really isn't a choice that needs to be made here or that we might already know what we want to do. What might actually be needed is courage and confidence, to own what we actually want. And if our gut is saying that we don't wanna go to this party, then perhaps we should skip it.

Let's try a second reading. Same scenario, different cards:

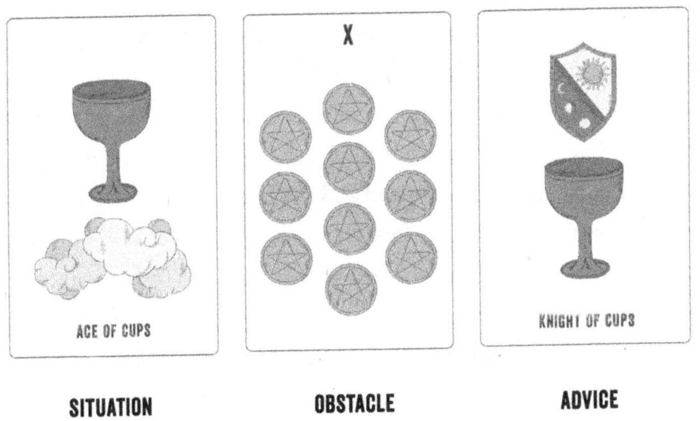

Again, take some time to carefully consider this reading. How does each card answer the question of its position? Do any of these cards confuse you? How would you read this spread for yourself?

This first card, in the position of situation, brings a very different energy from the other sample reading that we looked at. The Ace of Cups often speaks to a new emotional beginning or a gift from the suit of water. We could see this card as a potential door opening, even the turning over of a new leaf when it comes to the emotional and relational lens that we are so often using when we consider the suit of water. But the Ace of Cups also tends to acknowledge the full scope of potential within the suit: meaning the good and the bad, the hard and the useful, the challenging and the comforting. I personally would read the Ace of Cups in the situation position as pointing to the fact that this party could be whatever we make of it. The emotions and intentionality and willingness to engage that we bring with us to approaching the event could shape the outcome of what the event ultimately is for us.

The second card, the Ten of Pentacles, is in the position of an obstacle. And we tend to read the Ten of Pentacles as this card of stability, comfort, pleasure, abundance, and having absolutely everything that we need in order to feel safe, secure, and cared for. If we're approaching this reading from the lens of having to go to a place where we don't feel safe, this obstacle card could indicate that we don't have a very good read on that situation and that this is actually a safer place for us than we might recognize. But Tens in the tarot also can really speak to something being pushed to its limit or leveling up, and so this card could alternatively represent that there's an abundance of responsibility or even pressure that is contributing to this feeling of obstacle. Family obligations, family needs, and family expectations can all be really heavy and complicated to navigate. So this obstacle could be less about a literal feeling of not being safe or welcome and be much more about not wanting to let anyone down.

The final card is the advice card, and this is the Knight of Cups. Similarly to the Priestess, there's an argument that this card really means trusting your gut. But while the Priestess is a Two card and has this energy of stability and calmness and contemplation and awareness, Knights are a little bit more frenetic and a little bit more restless. I see Knights as Three cards: figures that are eager to quest and adventure, that aren't afraid to take big chances, people who are willing to wear their hearts on their sleeve. The Knight of Cups in particular is willing to take chances around relationships and is eager to trust their intuition to guide them down unknown but exciting paths.

While the first reading using this spread seemed like it was warning against conflict, frustration, and a lack of safety, this second reading feels quite a bit different. Same situation, same spread, but very different cards that lead to a very different potential outcome. These cards seem to hold a lot of possibility, particularly around the idea of a new beginning, active growth, and the surprise that can happen when we take a chance. Unlike with the first reading, I see this second one as an invitation to consider the good that might happen at this party. There may be potential for new relationships to blossom, changes in feelings around safety or stability, and perhaps even opportunities for emotional chances that lead to new connections, support, or discoveries.

At the end of the day, each reading still leaves the choice of whether or not to attend the party up to you, the querent. You still have free will and can make this decision for yourself. But each reading offers a different set of perspectives on what the real obstacle is, as well as different advice for what to do based on that information. While each final card in these readings holds a lot of space for doing what feels best for us, the two readings overall might lead us to different conclusions. They each tell a very different story.

PART THREE

WRITING SPREADS

At some point, using the tarot spreads that you find out in the world might not be enough. You may end up frustrated when you can't find a spread that addresses what you need, especially if you want to pull cards for a specific situation that is unique and individual to you. Or you might want something very particular from your reading that none of the general spreads that you can find seem to address.

General spreads are wonderful and are often incredibly useful. But if you're itching to try your hand at creating your own custom spreads from scratch, I've got you covered. Read on.

What Does It Mean to Write a Tarot Spread?

Writing a tarot spread means deciding for yourself what the spread looks like, how it's organized, how it works, and what it explores—along with what it leaves out. This task includes everything from deciding how many cards are going to be used to writing the different positions that will be included. When you write a tarot spread, you get to decide every aspect of what the reading will look like. But it also means that the responsibility for ensuring that the spread is logical, usable, and appropriate falls onto you—which could be exciting or could be stressful, based on your personality and level of experience as a tarot reader.

To write our own tarot spread is to create the blueprint for the reading that we want to do or to create a structured format that we can use in future readings. It is taking more control over the flow of the reading itself and creating positions that will work together to tell a compelling story; offer needed insight; or help us explore a decision, challenge, or truth in more depth.

Writing a tarot spread is the process of creating a new layout to be used in either a highly specific or more generally applicable situation. And while we'll mainly be exploring writing tarot spreads for yourself in this portion of the book, tarot spreads can also be written for specific individuals, clients, or even broader communities. Whether they're general or specialized, this is a process that takes time, creativity, patience, and a willingness to learn.

Why Would We Need to Write Our Own Spreads?

No matter who you are, your life, your personality, your experiences, and your dreams are unique to you. No one has ever existed that is exactly like you. And isn't that wonderful?

Most tarot spreads that are released into the world are designed for a general audience, to be accessible and useful to as many people as possible in as many different situations as possible. This includes spreads published in books and newsletters, shared through social media, or passed on through practitioners. There's no shortage of tarot spreads in the world, and new ones are written every single day. Sometimes, though, we want a tarot spread that is more personalized, that addresses our unique concerns, that lets us ask highly specific or individual questions. Sometimes we can't find a general spread that really gets to the heart of the matter, that addresses the kinds of concerns we have. Sometimes, especially if we've been reading tarot for a long time, we start to appreciate specific positions or card prompts and understand more clearly which styles of tarot spreads serve us the best.

The more we use tarot spreads, the more we start to develop personal preferences around them. While sometimes that translates to finding tarot writers whose work we really vibe with, and who write spreads that we use frequently, sometimes this can also mean that we want to be empowered to create our own spreads, ones that reflect those preferences.

There's no shame in wanting to write your own spreads. When I first started to consider creating a spread of my own, it was after spending hours trying to find a spread that really got to the heart of a sticky situation that I was navigating. Try as I might, no matter how many great spreads I found, none of them really addressed my main questions or offered the kinds of insights that I was seeking. While I was nervous to dive into this new technique, I badly wanted to lean on my cards for support. Not knowing anyone who wrote tarot spreads personally at that time, I didn't really have an option but to write my own—so I did. And while that first reading didn't go particularly well, it did teach me firsthand just how important it is to use care, intentionality, and restraint when writing tarot spreads.

I know that this is likely not an unfamiliar situation. For many of us, the hours spent searching for the "perfect" spread to suit our needs could be better spent developing a spread of our own. And while it takes time to build skill in this area, once you start to create spreads, once you learn what works best for you and begin to build a system for putting spreads together that you love, it becomes a bit intoxicating.

There can be real power, real joy, real magic, in writing a spread that is perfectly designed to suit our needs. Plus, there's a lot of satisfaction in using those spreads in our own readings, especially when they really work the way that we want them to.

When Should We Write Our Own Spreads?

We've already talked about how tarot spreads are really great for moments when you want specificity in your readings, when you want to drill down on a particular topic or ask a specific kind of question. But creating a new spread takes this process a step further. When you write your own tarot spread, you can tailor it to exactly what your needs are—and can ensure that the conversation you have with your cards goes in the direction that you want it to go.

Writing your own spreads is also a really great general exercise for developing your skills as a tarot reader. Using tarot spreads is absolutely not mandatory for being a skilled, talented, or experienced tarot reader—which means that writing your own spreads isn't either. But if you do want to eventually move into reading tarot professionally or want to feel as though you can read about anything you want to read about, learning the skill of writing your own tarot spreads is a great way to practice working with them from another angle.

Even if you ultimately decide that you don't want to be constantly writing original tarot spreads for your readings, exploring what it looks like for you to write your own spreads can help you understand how spreads function and work for you, as well as clarify what kinds of spreads are your preferred layouts to work with.

Here's a sample scenario: Let's say that you want to pull some cards around a new job offer that's come in. There are pros and cons to your current position and company, but you've been itching for some new opportunities, and this job possibility sounds pretty good on paper. You're hoping that a tarot reading can help you figure out whether to take the new job or to stay at your old one.

You could keep it simple and shuffle up the deck, asking for general insights into what this new job would look like and whether it would be a good fit. You could pull cards in response to this question, and see what comes up, reading in a more general and open style. You could even ask more questions after this initial pull, drawing more cards to answer those follow-up questions or to clarify the answers. And this is a perfectly legitimate way to read the cards.

But what if you have more specific questions? What if you want to look more closely at your current position, acknowledging existing frustrations or limits, and also gain insights into the new job? What if you want to ask the cards about your potential new boss and coworkers, the financial stability this new job might offer, how it might impact your nonworking hours, what it might provide in terms of career growth? By writing a tarot spread specifically for your situation, you could assign a card position to every one of those questions and ensure that you receive answers for each facet of this question. The process of writing that spread might even help you clarify what's most important to you around considering this new job, as (for example) you might realize that since the job is largely independent, the people you work with won't have a major impact on your daily routine, or that your own career growth is already so stagnant that any potential for movement is a step in the right direction. Just thinking through which positions you'd want to include in the spread and which ones you choose to leave out can also help you figure out your own priorities *before you've even done the tarot reading!*

Both methods will likely give you a clear result and help you have a good conversation with your cards. However, where a general, more open-ended reading is useful for broad topics and looser exploratory questions, writing a spread will help give specificity and definition to a tarot reading and provide more detailed answers on a variety of related aspects of the overall situation.

When Should We *Not* Write Our Own Spreads?

Of course, there are times when writing a spread for ourselves might not be the best tactic. The first and most definitive moment to avoid writing a spread is if you do not yet know what you want to know. If you cannot articulate what you're looking for from the cards or cannot break that need down into distinct questions or prompts, trying to write a spread could become a very frustrating effort. You might be better served by journaling or talking to a friend, not only from a support standpoint but also because sometimes simply talking about or through the situation to yourself or to another person can help you understand what would be the most helpful for you and what might be useful to examine through the lens of the tarot.

Writing a spread can also be difficult if you don't use them in readings very often or haven't yet found a formula, layout, or general approach for using spreads that you know you like. There's absolutely nothing wrong with writing more open-ended or general spreads. Sometimes the simplest spreads can be the most poignant! But if you tend to be disappointed in your readings with spreads, or if you don't have a type of spread that you know you enjoy, trying to write one without any kind of positive or appealing example may be very difficult. You don't need to force yourself to use a tarot tool or technique that doesn't work for you! So, if spreads don't really suit your reading style, or you find yourself with more questions than answers after using them, writing your own spread might not feel any different than using one you found through a different resource.

The other time that I recommend not writing your own spread is if you're in a hurry to pull cards. Sometimes we're anxious or eager to get to reading and are so focused on getting our hands on our cards and receiving some insights that writing a spread feels like the last thing we want to do. With practice, writing a tarot spread can become second nature and takes only a few moments to finish. But when you're getting started or just learning the process, creating a tarot spread from scratch might take a long time and could require a few tests, rounds of edits, or other adjustments. If you're not interested in putting in the time and effort to get the spread in a good place before using it, writing a tarot spread might feel like more effort than it's worth, and you might be better served by using a general spread that already exists.

Tarot often has a reputation as a very serious, introspective, intense tool. It certainly can be! But anytime we're feeling particularly activated, stressed, nervous, upset, frustrated, angry, or otherwise not our best selves, reaching for the cards on our own might not be the first solution I would recommend. Trying to write a tarot spread in a very charged state—especially if it's a practice we're not particularly familiar or comfortable with—can only make those heightened feelings harder to navigate.

In addition to being intense or truthful, tarot can also be fun, creative, relaxing, inspiring, or hilarious, depending on the energy that we are bringing to our readings. If you really want to try writing your own spreads, but you aren't sure where to start, how to do it, or what you're looking for, start with something that is silly, light, or easy. I've written spreads for everything from processing major grief to deciding what to eat for dinner, and the process is essentially the same. But a spread with a premise or positions that make me laugh can be a lot more lighthearted to work on.

If you're hankering to learn how to write a spread, start with something low-key and low-stakes, rather than diving headfirst into the biggest, most serious and intense topic you can think of. It's a great way to learn; plus you'll have some fun spreads to play with whenever you want.

How Do We Write Tarot Spreads? Where Do We Even Start?

Before jumping headfirst into writing a tarot spread, we'll need to do a bit of preparation. Even with a lighthearted practice spread, it's important to know what your goals are, what your preferences are, and what your concerns are. No matter what you want to write a spread about, take the time to go through these three steps first, even if you don't spend hours working through these ideas.

First, let's start with **goals**. These are the objectives of your spread, the reasons that you're writing it, the shit you hope to make happen within the reading. In other words, your goal is your main question, the theme of your reading, the reason you want to do this. What is the main purpose of this tarot spread? Where is the need for this particular reading coming from? What do you want to accomplish with this spread? What conversation do you want this spread to facilitate?

Your goal is your why. Why are you writing this spread? Why are you turning to the cards for answers or support? Why are you here, now, putting this layout together? What is the underlying need or desire that is driving this activity forward? What are you looking for?

This step includes paying attention to spread categories, something we covered previously. Spread categories are an aspect of a spread's purpose or function—the thing that we will walk away from the reading carrying. Some spreads are focused on *advice*, others are written to provide *insight*, and still others are created for *support*. Regardless of whether or not you tend to gravitate toward a particular category in general, it's important to consider if you hope to receive one, two, or all three of these gifts from the cards as part of your reading, as this will help you ensure that you include clear positions for these kinds of results while crafting your spread.

Next, consider your **preferences**. They are what you know about yourself, your likes and dislikes, and your needs when it comes to tarot spreads. Every tarot reader has different tastes when it comes to their spreads, their readings, and their tarot work. Do you love a long spread with lots of positions, covering a question from many angles all at once, giving you plenty to chew on? Or do you prefer a quick-and-dirty spread that gets to the heart of the question without a lot of fanfare? Do you like prompts that are questions, statements, single words, or vibes? Does having the spread in a graphic or visual format feel necessary for you to be able to really understand it, or do you prefer writing the positions out in a line? Do you like working with a significator card or having a specific card pulled out to help shape your reading?

It's okay if every one of these questions doesn't feel relevant to the spread you want to write. But consider what you generally like in your tarot spreads: what you gravitate toward, what feels comfortable, what opens up new ways of thinking or provides the kind of support you're craving. Which preferences might be the most useful to keep in mind during the crafting of this particular spread? What do you want to make sure is included in the format, method, or style?

Additionally, consider these questions: Is this a spread that you want to be highly specific or more general? Are you writing this spread with the intention of using it many times or for using it just once? Are the questions that you want to be addressed in this spread ones that you ask your cards a lot? Would it be worthwhile to make this particular spread a bit more general so that you can use it over and over again, or would you prefer to have it be something that feels uniquely crafted for a specific occasion?

Lastly, before writing a new tarot spread, I always like to check in with myself about **concerns**. Is there anything I'm afraid of exploring during this reading? Is there a topic, question, truth, or uncertainty that's hovering around the edges, something that I might need to acknowledge? Is there something that I'm trying to avoid? Are there fears that might impact the way that I use this spread?

It is perfectly okay to have things that you don't want to be covered or discussed in a tarot reading. Often when we come to the tarot, we're looking for assurance, comfort, support, encouragement, or advice—ways of taking control, reminders that we are worthy, insights into what may happen, or other truths that can help soothe frayed nerves or calm our fears. We might feel really stressed, or really stuck, and are hoping that a reading will provide clarity or concrete advice. But I think it's important, especially when writing a spread for our own use, that we acknowledge those sticky aspects before diving into creation. It's just as essential to recognize what we aren't interested in exploring as it is to know what we want to cover.

Note that this recognition of concerns doesn't always have to be something traumatic or anxiety-based, buried deep in your subconscious. This might be as simple as not wanting to dive into certain kinds of questions! For example, if you're writing a spread for getting through a creative block, you might know that you want to avoid thinking about past times when you felt creatively stuck, since that can send you spiraling. You might know going in that you are far more interested in focusing on your present challenges. That's completely fine! Giving yourself space to honor that concern instead of trying to avoid it will help you write a spread that feels safe, focused, and intentional. The act of thinking through and naming any fears or discomforts gives you time to pay attention to concepts, questions, or topics that you know that you are not interested in exploring during this reading.

The point of all of this discussion is to write a spread that truly works for you and that includes ensuring that you have taken the time to understand what it is you want, what it is you don't want, and what preferences you have about how you'll get there.

What Does a Well-Written Tarot Spread Include?

From my perspective, a thoughtful, functional, and usable tarot spread includes a few key components:

Prompts. These are the positions that serve as the main content for the reading, that offer a question for the tarot deck to answer. Prompts should be clear, should be relatively concise, and should make sense to you as a reader. If you don't know what the prompt means, it's going to be very hard to work with! You can think of the prompts in a spread like stepping stones on a path: these are the beats in the conversation, the points that are made in a debate, the logical facts that are shared in an argument. Prompts are where you plant your feet, the solid ground that provides the foundation for the steps you take in the reading.

Flow. This is how the positions work together to create a cohesive story, argument, perspective, insight, or offer of advice. Tarot spreads should feel logical, like each card is building to the next one and like each prompt works with the others to provide something specific. Sticking with our stepping-stone path metaphor, flow represents how close each stone is to the next and how easy it is to access one prompt from another. If the stones are too far apart, we may find ourselves trying to fill in logical gaps or even getting lost in between steps. But if they're too close together, we may feel as though we're just walking in circles or stuck in place. Flow is all about keeping the spread moving, while keeping our vision for where we're going clear.

Sometimes flow is literally represented within the spread graphics and images, giving us an additional insight into how each position builds on the next. The ways that the cards are laid out can provide clues into how each card connects to the others in the spread. In a three-card layout, for example, laying the cards out in different ways helps us to visually observe the relationships between the prompts

EXAMPLE 1:

EXAMPLE 2:

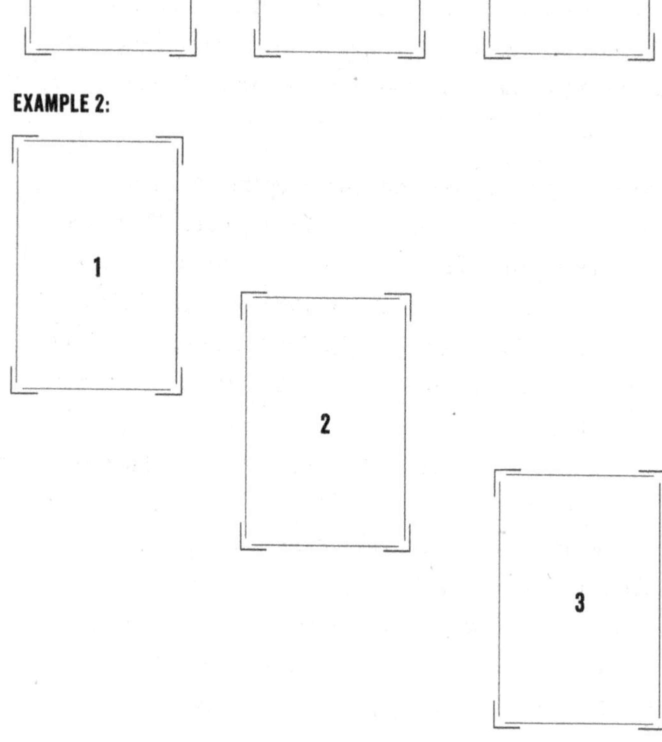

EXAMPLE 3:

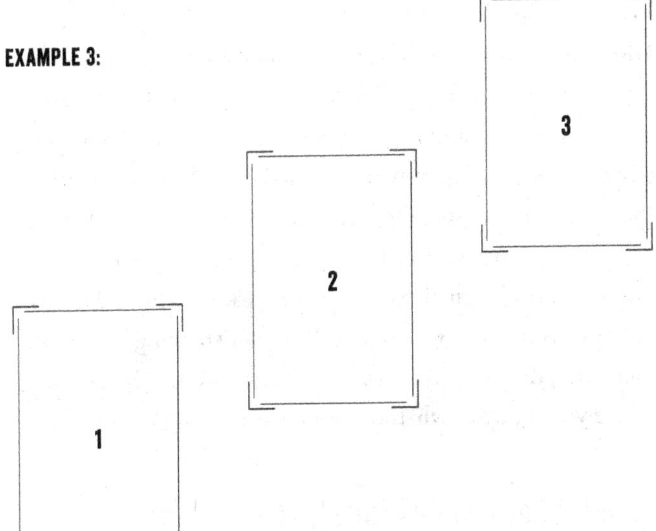

EXAMPLE 4:

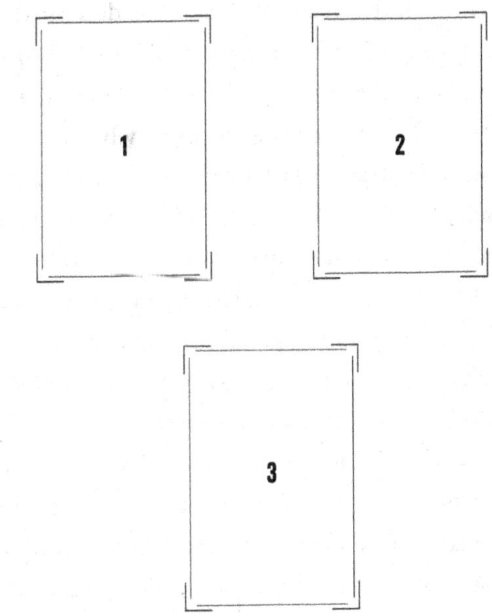

Objective. Finally, tarot spreads should have a clear goal or a vision for where they are leading us. Some spreads are just meant to be vibes and may not have a particular end point like advice for a next step or help with making a decision—and that's okay! Other spreads may have an obvious destination, with each prompt leading us to a specific finish line. Both kinds of spreads can give deep, potent readings, but we need to know which type we're using. With our stepping-stone path metaphor, the objective is where the path ultimately leads us: where we end up or what we have been working toward.

Okay, but What Do I *Do*? How Do I Write My First Tarot Spread?

Starting to write your first tarot spread can be intimidating, even after working through the necessary steps just described. How many positions should you write? What do you include? How specific can you be? How do you know if the spread will be effective for you?

The answer, as with basically everything when it comes to tarot, is practice, care, and patience. There are many ways to approach writing tarot spreads, and I will share some of my favorite methods here. But I highly encourage you to play around with different formats, different lengths, and different focuses. Test the various approaches presented here, writing sample spreads on multiple topics using each method. See what feels good, what feels weird, what you might want to try out, and what you might want to toss.

My first spreads were longer (meaning that they had more card positions) than the ones I typically write now and had a lot of redundancy, which made for confusing readings. It's taken time for me to figure out the length of spreads that I prefer, the types of positions that work well for me, and the flow and format that I prefer. While I will share my experience and knowledge with you here, your ultimate preferences may vary wildly from my own. That's perfectly okay! You are your own reader, and the beauty of writing your own spreads is that you can ensure that they suit you, your reading styles, and your unique preferences.

Keep in mind that writing a tarot spread is sometimes an instinctive, intuitive process, and other times it might require a lot of practical effort. For me, it's usually a mix of both—experience and intuition tangling up together. Don't be afraid to make some strong or weird choices, and remember that you can always try something new. Spreads are not static, and you can change or adjust them as many times as you like. Release any pressure to do this perfectly the first time, and instead try to have fun with this process. Play around, trust your gut, and see what happens. You're not getting graded, and the tarot police are not going to come to your house and take your cards away. See what works for you, and run with it.

How Do I Test a Spread?

Learning how to test a tarot spread without getting emotionally invested in the cards that you pull is a critical skill in spread writing, especially when you're learning to create new spreads. But it can feel stressful sometimes to be doing a full tarot reading just to test the functionality of a spread! So how do we do it?

There are a few ways that you can test a tarot spread that's in development. If you're writing a layout that's fairly simple and general, and you feel fairly confident that it follows a clear path that will give you the kinds of answers that you're looking for, you can test the spread with a full tarot reading for yourself. This is best done on a topic that is fairly low stakes, but as you develop in your skills and experience, you may be able to do a more intensive reading with a new spread and still get great results.

However, my best advice is this: Test your spread with a reading for a hypothetical person. Be clear with your tarot card deck that this reading will be a test (I literally say this out loud to my deck when testing a spread!). Then make up an imaginary friend or a fictional client, write them a quick backstory and question, and perform the reading for that situation. Pay attention to how each position feels, how the cards respond to that position, and how the overall reading flows together.

If you like, you can name this person and have them be your regular fake test subject that you read for whenever you're tweaking or testing a new tarot spread. You could also read for a favorite character from a book or piece of media, if you don't want to make up an entire imaginary friend. You do you.

Don't try to be sneaky and make this hypothetical person's problem or question exactly like yours so that you can just do a reading for yourself by proxy. The point here is to *distance* yourself from the cards that come forward so that you can assess whether or not the spread functions the way that you want it to without getting activated or emotional about the answers that come forward. It'll be easier to be objective about the spread itself, rather than the answers, if you are reading for a person who does not exist.

Once the reading is complete, be honest with yourself about how well the spread worked. Were there any positions that seemed good in theory but were confusing to read with? Did any positions end up feeling redundant or too similar to one another and could potentially be removed? When you look at the full reading, does it feel as though another position might add some additional clarity? What is the final message of the reading, and how does the final prompt wrap up the messages from the cards?

Don't be shy about testing your spreads. Sometimes you may need to do a few sample readings in order to figure out what needs to be adjusted!

How Can I Write a Practice Spread?

One of the easiest ways to start writing original spreads is by whipping up a spread as a practice exercise and intentionally trying out a few methods for creation to see what resonates and comes the most naturally to you. You might use different methods for different spreads on different days, depending on what you're feeling. Or you might find a method that suits you well and toss the rest, always following the same technique. Do whatever works for you. Testing each of the following three methods will teach you about your own writing style and help you learn what works best for you—and what doesn't.

Note that each of the methods I describe assumes that you have already gone through the steps to clarify your goals, preferences, and concerns. I've associated each method with a particular major arcana archetype to help you understand the general vibe of each process, but please feel free to take liberties, test your own methods, and leave anything that doesn't work for you. Writing spreads is an art, not a science, and there's no need for you to try and exactly replicate what I've outlined here if it doesn't feel right. There are many, many ways to write spreads, and I'm not including every single way that tarot writers create layouts here—just a few tried-and-true methods to get you started, along with some exercises that offer additional ways to develop your spreads.

To write your first practice spread, I recommend choosing a simple, general theme. Pick something that you will use on a regular basis, rather than a one-off spread for a highly specific situation. My favorite suggestions include a spread for your mornings or evenings, a spread on embracing the energy of a specific tarot archetype, or a spread for celebrating an aspect of yourself. Each has plenty of room for adjustment, and you can write a completely different version of each spread using each of the three methods here. You also might find that you love all three versions for different reasons! The stakes are low with these because they're practical without being too tender, easy to test, and lovely to reuse.

If you're ready to create your first spread, choose your topic, take a few moments to consider your goals, preferences, and concerns for that topic. Then dive into each of the following three creation methods.

Method One: The Way of the Magician

The Magician method is all about opening your mind to possibility, diving in headfirst, and seeing what comes up when you take off all the filters. This method is essentially brainstorming until things start to click—writing out aspects of the spread and then eventually piecing together your favorite bits into one cohesive layout. If you're someone who often feels pulled in a lot of directions, like you have so many ideas they have trouble finding their form or like you could write ten spreads on this topic instead of just one, the Magician method might feel particularly good for you.

I highly recommend grabbing a journal, opening a fresh digital document or note, or turning on a voice recorder. This is about getting as many ideas out of your brain as possible; having a space to dump those ideas will help you sort through them later. In this instance there's no such thing as too much, so go wild. Record your ideas until you don't have any more.

Begin by considering **every aspect of this particular topic that might be worthy of exploration, or of interest**. (And yes, that is a big idea! That's the point!) What are the various angles of this situation, idea, dream, or question that you could use the cards to address? What is most exciting to you? What comes forward right away when you consider the topic you've chosen for your spread?

Don't worry about writing out these ideas as exact spread positions just yet—no need to get ahead of yourself. Instead, just record various questions or curiosities that could help give this situation more shape, insight, or perspective. Consider the different angles you could take. Jot down everything that comes to mind.

To give you an example: if I wanted to write a tarot spread about stepping into the Fool's energy, I might start by listing out various characteristics of this card that I want to understand more deeply, activate within myself, or learn to navigate:

- Curiosity
- Desire
- New beginnings
- Untapped potential
- Rebellion
- Doing something unexpected
- Dreams
- Lack of experience

- Disruption
- Leaving something behind
- Starting a new path
- Exploration
- Discovery
- Following your arrow
- Trusting your gut
- Cravings

Once you've written down a bunch of different ideas, keywords, or angles that come to mind around your chosen topic, start to consider how your list might bring up certain **questions**. Your spread will have a driving question, of course (for a general morning spread, it might be as simple as "How can I prepare for the day ahead?" while for my Fool archetype example, it might be "How can I embrace the Fool's energy right now?"), but questions can often lead to more questions.

To continue with this Fool example, I might write down general questions that come up when I think about the Fool, questions that I might ask this figure, ask about this figure, or want to know more about this figure. These questions don't necessarily have to directly connect to my spread, but they might come up based on the keywords and ideas that I've already listed, or serve as extensions of the topics I've already come up with:

- Who is the Fool?
- What might the Fool have to teach me right now?
- How would the Fool behave in this situation?

- What is the Fool really good at?
- What does the Fool need to learn?
- How is the Fool wise?
- What drives the Fool's curiosity?
- What supports the Fool's courage?
- What activates the Fool's rebellion?
- Whom might the Fool look to for support?
- What is the Fool leaving behind?
- What is the Fool reaching for?
- What does being the Fool feel like?
- What is a past time that I've felt like the Fool?
- How do I activate the Fool's energy?
- What is something I can do to feel like the Fool?

Now we're getting somewhere. These questions can help us get to the heart of what we're really looking for from our reading. At this point, look back through your lists so far, and see which topics and questions jump out. Which keywords, phrases, or meanings feel the most aligned with what you want this particular spread to explore? Which questions resonate the most, questions that you might like to find answers to using this spread?

If you like, you can make a new list separating out the topics and questions that you want to use in your spread. Take as long with this process as you like, and record anything that feels relevant. Once you have a smaller grouping of chosen ideas, take a few moments to look at your selections. What do they have in common? Which themes are you circling around?

My personal preferences for spreads are short and sweet (three- to four-card spreads), using either short statements or simple questions. For me, that means the next step in this process looks like converting these words and questions into spread positions. For you, that might look different, but if my tarot spreads resonate with you at all, I encourage you to try this method first. You can always repeat it with your own preferences later.

Look at your consolidated list, and try **converting some or all of these items into spread positions.** Don't worry yet about choosing which ones you want to use. For now, just shift as many of them as you like into spread positions that resonate with your own preferences.

For my example, I'm converting various statements or phrases that could be helpful in different ways when it comes to my specific topic of the Fool. Remember that spreads can offer clarity and insight, advice and action items, support and encouragement, or anything else that you might be looking for from a reading. I like to list various questions or prompts that address these different needs, based on the previous lists, and also include at least one prompt for each spread category as a potential outcome or final card, like this:

- Something to be curious about
- Something to explore
- A dream that is revealing itself
- A truth to acknowledge
- A desire to celebrate
- A potential path forward

- A next step
- Something to embrace
- Something that is beginning
- Something to release
- Something to leave behind
- A wisdom you have
- A question to ask
- A topic to explore
- An impulse to trust
- A warning
- A compliment
- A suggestion
- Advice

Now you've got the potential bones of your spread. Pay attention to the prompts that sing to you right now, but don't cross anything out or toss any ideas away. You may want to use these lists for reference later, and having ideas listed already can make future spread writing even easier. Instead, **make a new, consolidated list** of the phrases, questions, keywords, or ideas that most appeal to you in this moment. Try to keep this new list to ten or fewer, particularly if your goal is a three- or four-card spread.

Once you have a handful of prompts, **consider what story they are telling**. Are there similarities between them? Are they connected in any particular way? How might one prompt lead into another naturally, telling a story and offering insights that dovetail nicely into one another? Which ones coordinate, support each other, connect?

This is a moment to listen to your intuition, to pay attention to which questions or categories you feel most drawn to. It's okay if you don't know if a prompt is perfectly "right" just yet. This step is just about paying attention to the aspects of your question that feel the most pressing, the most central to your query.

If it's helpful, at this point you can write down a **thesis statement** or general summary of the prompts that feel the most relevant and compare that to your original goal for this spread. When you thread these consolidated list pieces together, what are they ultimately getting at? What are they seeking? Where do they direct your focus and attention? And what might they result in?

For my Fool spread example, I might decide that for stepping into the Fool's energy, I really like these specific prompts and questions from my earliest lists:

- A dream that is revealing itself
- Something that is beginning
- What might the Fool have to teach me right now?
- A question to ask
- Advice
- How do I activate the Fool's energy?

In looking at these chosen prompts, I can see that I'm really gravitating toward insights and advice. These prompts are about clarity and new information, wanting to better understand what I'm feeling drawn to and what I might want to begin. But I also see multiple prompts for advice and activating, asking for tangible ways that I can find Fool energy within myself. That tells me that I really want some practical insights and that I should make sure to have prompts from each category in the final spread.

The last step is **putting it all together**, and this may feel kind of like assembling a puzzle. You've just got to try out different things and see what feels good. Some people like to write each of the possible prompts on scraps of paper or index cards and physically move them around on a surface until they've found the story, arc, narrative, or flow that resonates the most deeply. Others write down prompts in different orders until they find one they like. You might have a more slow and steady method, choosing prompts for specific beats of the spread and then filling in the gaps to ensure a cohesive flow.

To return to the Fool spread example one final time, I might decide that my first draft spread looks like this:

something the Fool has to teach me right now / something that is beginning / something I can do to activate the Fool's energy within myself

Whatever your method, don't rush this part. Try different prompts, mix up the order, or even scribble down new ones if inspiration strikes. Play around until you find one that resonates.

Congratulations, you've got a practice spread! The only thing left to do is to **test it**. Grab your tarot deck and use the spread for a reading, either for yourself or for that imaginary friend I mentioned earlier. Pay attention to how each position feels when you're using it and how the overall reading feels. Are there moments when you felt stuck? Does a position feel repetitive or confusing? Do the prompts flow into one another, each naturally setting up the next position? Record your experience with this spread.

Sometimes, after the first reading, it's very obvious what needs to shift: You may need to rewrite a position to be more clear or focused, or you may need to loosen it up a little so that it's easier to read. Sometimes just swapping the order of two positions makes all the difference. You may find that you have more prompts than you really need for a clear reading or that the spread could use another position or two.

Keep tweaking and testing. You might need to use the spread a few times to get it right! And if you find yourself getting frustrated, take a breather and walk away for a time. It's amazing how often just taking a little space can bring new clarity.

As you get more comfortable writing spreads, especially if this becomes your favorite creation method, you may be able to skip the list steps altogether and move straight to the thesis statement. Or you may find that you prefer to keep adding to your lists, making a giant reference of prompts that you can use over and over for various spreads.

Keeping a written list of these prompts is an easy way to manage them. But if you're someone who likes a more hands-on approach, consider purchasing a pack of blank playing cards or using plain index cards. Write a question or prompt on each one (use both sides if you have ones that are very similar, that you would be unlikely to use in the same spread), and keep this pack as a regular tool you can pull out whenever you want to play with putting together a new spread. This way, you can arrange the cards differently and mix up the positions to see what feels best. If you try this approach, I highly recommend using different colors for the ink or the card stock for different positions, or labeling them with stickers so that you can easily find prompts that fall into different categories. This approach can be completely tailored to you and your preferences! If you always like to have an advice position in your spreads, for example, make those cards stand out in some way so that they're easy to find in your stack.

Method Two: The Way of the Hierophant

Another way to write a tarot spread is by researching other spreads that you like or by making notes about the kinds of positions you prefer. As I've said before, the more you know about the kinds of spreads you like to use in your practice, the easier it becomes to take those spreads apart and replicate their methodology for yourself. By taking the time to closely look at a spread that you know you love reading with, you can build on that method to create new spreads for yourself. If you're someone who tends to get caught up in worries about "doing something wrong" or are concerned that your original spread won't work, you might find this a comfortable and approachable method. Tap into your inner Hierophant and get ready to do some research.

To begin this method, **gather together some of your favorite tarot spreads**. Unlike with Method One, this is a place for discernment: Don't pull together every single tarot spread you've ever used, or you'll likely get overwhelmed. Instead, choose two or three tarot spreads that you've used multiple times. If you tend to use your spreads only once, then choose a tarot spread you've used that deeply resonated, felt supportive or encouraging, or provided the kinds of insights that are similar to the spread you want to create.

Once you have a couple of spreads that you love, take some time to **look at these spreads carefully**. Take notes on what you find. Do the spreads have anything in common, like the number of cards or the position type or the overall vibe? Do they all focus on similar things, like offering advice, creating space for insights, providing encouragement, or urging clarity? If you're someone who records your readings, I highly recommend that you look back on readings that you've done with these spreads or with spreads that are similar. Which positions feel the most comfortable for you? Which ones challenge you in a good or helpful way? Are there particular kinds of positions that feel harder for you to understand or connect with?

> Note: Please be aware that I am absolutely not advocating for the stealing of other people's original work. There is a big difference between finding inspiration in someone's structured methods and passing off someone else's spread as your own, feeding someone else's tarot spread into a generative AI chatbot to "rewrite" it, or otherwise pretending you wrote something that you didn't create. Many of us share original tarot spreads for use in tarot communities, free of charge, so there is a huge variety of free tarot resources available. Don't be disrespectful to this kind of specialized labor or spit in the face of creators' generosity. If you want to use or share someone else's tarot spread, do so! But don't pretend that it's your own, and don't simply repackage or slightly edit a spread that someone else created and pretend that you wrote it from scratch.

Remember that the purpose here is not to make a spread that feels hard to use or that you don't particularly enjoy reading with. There's no shame in recognizing that some positions, questions, or types of prompts are hard for you to connect with, don't work with your reading style, or simply don't feel great. Being aware of those things can help you learn how to write spreads that will actually support your reading preferences! Take note of the positions you love, as well as the ones that may not have worked as well for you.

Once you've reflected on your favorite spreads, **make a list of the positions that you resonate with most.** If you prefer short spreads, this might mean that you have only a few listed, and if you're someone who loves a long spread, this list might be more intensive. The number of positions doesn't really matter because what I want you to do now is consider what those prompts accomplish in their respective spreads. If you find that a lot of your favorite types of prompts focus on a particular question, vibe, or result, that's an important clue to take note of. This might be the kind of position that you want in every spread you write or one that you can include regularly in your personal spreads.

Let's use this method to create another Fool spread, to give you an example. I've already written a number of spreads on the Fool over the years, but let's say that I want one that feels new and fresh. Here are three of my existing Fool spreads:

> ***What could the Fool teach me?***
> *something I've been craving / something that I've been afraid of / a way to embrace my natural courage*
>
> ***On Finding the Fool:***
> *a craving to acknowledge / a curiosity to indulge / a desire to chase*
>
> ***The Fool:***
> *a dream or idea that is taking shape / a fear or anxiety to recognize / a blessing or opportunity to embrace*

A few positions that I really love from these existing spreads are *a curiosity to indulge, a way to embrace my natural courage,* and *something that I've been afraid of.* But I also can see some potential other directions that a spread like this could go in and am interested in exploring what other themes a Fool spread could invite in.

Once you have some positions in mind, it's time to turn to your own spread. Remembering the kinds of prompts that you already like, consider how you might adjust or rewrite those favorites to suit your new spread. How can you replicate this kind of prompt for the topic you want to explore? Where might these prompts serve as inspiration for the kind of spread you want to create?

For example, if I'm ready to create a new Fool spread, I might start by just arranging the positions that I liked from my old spreads:

> *something that I've been afraid of / a curiosity to indulge / a way to embrace my natural courage*

I might feel as though this gets at where I want to go and use this spread as is! But if I wanted it to feel a bit more streamlined toward a different purpose, I could rewrite some of the positions like so:

> *a fear that's been impacting me / something I'm growing curious about / a way to push past my fears and chase after what I want*

I haven't completely lost the original meanings of the prompts, but I have adjusted them to have a bit more flow, move in a specific direction, and offer some additional clarity for the kind of spread that I'm creating. Because these are positions that I already know work for me, I can have a lot more confidence in this spread even as a first draft.

If you find yourself getting stuck with this method, make sure you understand *why* each position in the spread matters and *how* it's contributing to the overall reading. Having too many positions that dance around the same issue might feel like the spread is simply being thorough. But asking the same kind of question multiple times and getting cards that feel like they provide wildly different answers may lead to a murky, confusing, or frustrating reading experience. Don't be afraid to test your spread with multiple readings or to send it to a friend and have them try it too. Tweaks and adjustments are part of every tarot spread-writing process!

Each card's prompt should flow into one another, providing a setup for the next card. What story are you telling? What different aspects of the theme, situation, challenge, or question really need to be explored with the tarot? How does each card offer a new piece of the overall puzzle?

Method Three: The Way of the Priestess

The final method for spread writing that I want to share here is to try using the cards themselves to inspire and formulate the spread. This method is mentioned in Gail Fairfield's *Choice Centered Tarot* and explored in more depth through Rachel Pollack's *A Walk through the Forest of Souls.* Rather than trying to write every position yourself, this method involves pulling cards and then using those cards drawn to help us formulate additional questions. Depending on the cards that come forward, they can inspire specific kinds of questions or help to point us in a particular direction. This approach will likely be easier for those who are already fairly adept at reading tarot or who have specific relationships with the cards already, but it's not impossible for those who are newer to the practice. If you're comfortable with the tarot and understand how to listen to your intuition, if the Priestess is an archetype you feel aligned with, this method might really resonate for you.

> "Sometimes . . . I will ask the [querent] to mix the cards and choose, say, three or five cards. These cards will help us come up with valuable questions. So . . . when the Magician came up, it inspired the woman to ask the question, "What will my life look like if I really live out my dreams?" Once we have formulated the questions, we return the cards to the deck, and the woman mixes them once more in the usual way to discover what answers the cards can show her."
>
> (Pollack, *A Walk through the Forest of Souls,* Weiser Books, 2023, 29)

To try this method, consider the topic that you are trying to create a spread around. You may already have a position or two in mind but want to incorporate a few additional positions into the reading. Or you might just have a topic and not know where to go from there. Shuffle your tarot deck well, asking the cards to help you create some new questions. Then draw as many cards as you like to help you craft extra prompts. I recommend three to five cards, as Pollack does, but you can adjust this amount as needed. Look at the cards drawn, and consider how each card might offer a particular question that you can incorporate into the spread. What question does each card hold? How can you use them as inspiration for additional questions?

Here's an example: Say I'm trying to write a spread for supporting someone that I love who is going through a hard time. I might know that I'm seeking guidance and advice from the cards, both in the form of general insights into how to help them and also in some practical suggestions for tangible things that I can do. I might be sure that I want a position for something tangible that I can do to help my friend right now, but beyond that, I may not know where to go. The situation is so close to my heart that I can't quite formulate additional questions.

At this point, I grab my tarot deck, shuffle it well, and pull out five cards to help me formulate some additional questions. I draw the Four of Cups, the King of Wands, the Ten of Wands, the Two of Pentacles, and the Sun.

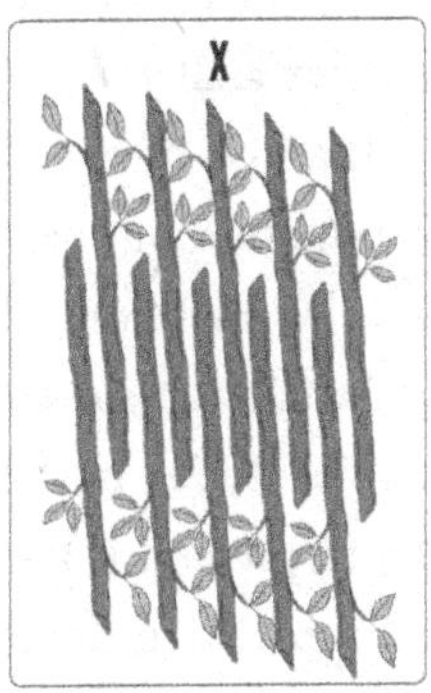

The Four of Cups might speak to containment or emotional boundaries—either my friend or I worrying about crossing emotional lines or opening up tenderness that won't have anywhere to go. This might inspire me to write a position like "How can I be sensitive to this person's fears?" or "What might be getting in the way of vulnerability?" The King of Wands is a card of bold risks and dynamic leadership, and may be a quality that could be really helpful in navigating a challenging situation. Just like the Sun, it speaks of abundance and community and of working together to make magic. Together, these cards might inspire questions like "What is something that my friend is doing really well that I can applaud?" or "Where is there something to celebrate in my friend's life? What in their life is better or stronger than they realize?"

The Ten of Wands and the Two of Pentacles both can speak to potential burnout or of trying to do many things at once. The Two of Pentacles might represent an energy of really crushing it, but in a way that isn't always sustainable. The Ten of Wands may have reached their goal, but there's nothing left to give. There are many different potential interpretations for these cards, but since they have this concept in common, that leads me to questions like "How can I offer material support to my friend?" or "What could I take off their plate?" But this also might indicate someone who is trying to find some power in a situation where they otherwise feel powerless, which could offer the question "How can I help my friend retake control?"

Using this method and gaining inspiration from the cards pulled in this example could result in a five-card spread that's something like this:

Ultimately, I might decide that including every one of these questions in one spread isn't necessary, or realize that my intuition is tugging me in a particular direction for the spread. Getting these suggestions directly from the cards is a powerful and helpful way to come at this theme or topic from a new angle and to formulate questions based directly off the chosen cards. It's also a great technique to fall back on if you're struggling to articulate a particular position that you know you want included in your layout.

A gentle reminder to not pull too many cards at once! As you've seen in the example, each card may inspire a number of questions, so don't bite off more than you can chew. Take your time with each card, writing down any relevant questions that come forward. Then look at the full list, identifying which cards feel the most useful, pressing, inspiring, or poignant. Try putting those questions together into a spread and testing it with a reading before pulling any additional cards.

Each of these three methods requires patience, attention, and a willingness to adapt. Don't rush these processes! Take your time, listen to your intuition, and don't be afraid to test things. Learning to write tarot spreads can be challenging, and everyone has their own style. If none of these methods work for you, that's okay. Chances are, just the practice of going through each of these methods will likely help you understand what *will* work for you.

EXERCISES AND RESOURCES

Learning to write tarot spreads absolutely takes practice, but the more you do it, the more it will start to flow naturally. And eventually, you might be able to write spreads that seem to barely require an effort at all!

1. Create a list of spread positions for yourself. One exercise I highly recommend is something that you may have already started doing in working with the sample spreads: listing potential spread positions that you might want to use. One way to do this is to look back at spreads you've enjoyed in the past, paying special attention to the prompts that resonate the most and adding those to your list. You can also just think about general positions that might be nourishing, encouraging, supportive, motivating, inspiring, clarifying, or otherwise helpful for you. Write them all down, from the very open to the wildly specific. This is not a place to be stingy. Even if an idea doesn't feel fully formed, write it down anyway.

Need a place to start? Here are a bunch of general prompts that I use regularly in my own original spreads:

- Something to know
- Something to learn
- Something to pay attention to
- Something to ask myself
- An important insight
- Necessary clarity
- A powerful revelation
- A secret that is being known
- A mystery to untangle
- Advice
- A next step
- Something to try
- Something to do
- Something to stop doing
- Something to keep doing
- A structure to incorporate
- A boundary to introduce

- A place to be less hard on yourself
- A way to show yourself grace
- A reminder
- A compliment
- A truth
- A gift
- Something beautiful you have to offer
- Something you're good at
- Something you're already doing well
- A way that you shine
- Something you already have
- Something you want
- Something you need
- Something you're afraid of
- Something you're excited about
- A strength
- A kind of magic
- An action
- An insight
- A way to take care of yourself

- A way to take care of others
- Something to leave behind
- Something to embrace
- Something to remember
- Something to release
- An emotion to face
- Something to own up to
- An obstacle
- A challenge
- Something you haven't realized
- Something you haven't noticed
- Something you haven't accepted
- An internal narrative
- Something to investigate
- Something to analyze
- Something to pursue
- An intention to set
- A journey to begin
- A potential outcome
- A pattern to recognize

- A shift that is present
- A transformation that is occurring
- Something to prepare for
- Something to focus on
- A boundary to set
- A structure to develop
- A rule to follow
- A rule to break
- A resource to activate
- A resource to gather
- A resource to utilize
- Guidance for a choice
- A direction to go
- A fear to address
- A way to stay grounded
- A way to be brave
- A way to ask for help
- A way to move forward
- Something unexpected

Which ones feel exciting to you? Which ones are you not interested in? What might open up a new conversation with your cards? This is just a starting point. Add as many as you like to this list, and toss out any that don't appeal.

Let this be an ongoing resource for you, a list that you can keep adding to and can draw from whenever you need fresh inspiration for a spread. If you're a visual or tactile person, I highly recommend buying a blank deck of cards or buying a pack of index cards and writing positions on individual cards. This way, you can draw randomly, rearrange positions, and play around with potential spreads. You can always add new positions as needed, but this can be a really inspiring way to try new layouts, adjust positions, or test potential spreads.

2. *Write some general spreads.* Practicing writing tarot spreads for different situations is really not something that there are any shortcuts for. You just have to keep trying and keep putting in the work. Testing these spreads is a really important piece of the puzzle because sometimes the spread will seem like it touches everything you want and addresses all of your various concerns and needs, but in practice it might become very clear after just a reading or two that the spread is missing something really important.

I highly recommend writing spreads that are general to start with rather than trying to get really specific right off the bat. However, I know that if you're reading this, you're likely already thinking about a highly specific and incredibly personal spread that you might want to write for your own personal use. Listen, I get it. Most of us who write a lot of tarot spreads started out on this path because we wanted layouts that we could not find out in the world. Once you start to acquire the skills required to create these spreads, you might want to immediately go wild and start writing as many spreads as you can.

When you're doing a reading for something that feels really tender, really personal, or really vulnerable, it's a lot harder to know if something is or is not working well. If you end up drawing cards that don't make sense to you, it can be a lot harder to parse whether you're struggling with the reading itself or whether the spread needs more tweaking. Doing readings around really sensitive topics is hard anyway, and if you're testing out a new spread that you've created for yourself, this can be a really challenging way to assess if you're writing spreads that are workable for you or not.

So with that in mind: Start small. Test your new skills with simple spreads like a morning routine spread or an evening reflection spread. Try creating a spread that's designed for checking in on your mind or body or heart. Experiment with spreads for creative projects or relaxing or taking care of yourself. These kinds of spreads can be as short or long as you like and can go very in depth or be very simple. Play around and try switching out different positions to see how it impacts the reading that you get from the spread. Note when the flow stagnates or feels off, as well as when a spread comes together with ease.

Need some prompts to get you started? Write spreads for the following topics:

- A morning organization spread
- An evening self-care spread
- A spread for checking in with your emotions
- A spread for feeling good about yourself
- A spread for making decisions
- A week-ahead spread

3. *Create spreads with friends.* Whether or not you're struggling with writing tarot spreads on your own, creating a spread with another person or a small group is a really fun way to expand your horizons and potentially play with spreads that you wouldn't normally try.

We all have patterns that we fall into, comfort zones that we prefer. But when collaborating with other people, even if it feels that we have very similar sensibilities when it comes to tarot, there are almost always surprises in what comes forward. Creating a spread with others can help you all build something new, inspiring, and supportive. Plus, after writing the spread together, you can test it with a group reading!

Where to start? First, discuss what kind of spread you want to write together. Is this a spread for providing concrete advice when making a decision or considering a sticky situation? Is this an encouraging spread, something to build you up or remind you of your magic, creativity, beauty, power, intelligence, and support? Is this an insight-oriented spread, one that might offer clarity or encourage a perspective shift? Is this a spread intended for the group to use together, or a spread that each person can use in their own practice? Make sure everyone involved in the writing of the spread is on the same page before you move forward.

There are plenty of ways to write a spread collaboratively, but my favorite method gives everyone a voice in the process. If you've already made a list of general tarot spread positions that you like, pull it out and show it to the people you're working with. Encourage them to make the same kind of list, either writing down positions that they know they like from memory or looking at tarot spreads they've found helpful in the past and noting their favorite prompts.

Once everyone has some potential pieces of the puzzle, have everyone choose at least one prompt from their list to add to the collaborative spread. Don't worry too much about making sure that these work together perfectly just yet. Instead, let everyone trust their instincts and select a position that they think is important to include. If you like, have everyone write down their position on a scrap of paper or index card.

Now comes the fun part: putting the positions together. Look at each position and consider where it might best fit in a spread. Is it a good introduction to the vibe of the reading? Does it set the tone, establish the topic, or create a baseline for deeper exploration? Choose the prompt that best opens the spread, that clears the way for the conversation to continue.

Then, consider which position might be the best fit for the final card in the spread—the conclusion, the advice, the last word. How do you want the spread to close? What prompt closes out the reading in a way that is supportive, encouraging, or motivating?

Finally, consider which prompts might help bridge the gap between the beginning and the ending. Which positions contribute to the conversation that you want to establish with the cards? Which questions are the most relevant? What helps you get from point A to point C, D, or even W? Remember that longer spreads aren't necessarily better or worse; it's more about paying attention to which positions feel relevant rather than getting too repetitive. If you look at the prompts you've all chosen and feel as though none of them quite work or you need more (or fewer) prompts to make the spread flow, go back to your lists. Include as many positions as you need.

Once you have a first draft of your spread, try it out! Do multiple readings with the same spread for different people who are present, and see how the spread might feel different for different folks, paying attention to how each position contributes to the overall flow and where edits might be helpful. Or, use the spread for a reading that applies to everyone in the group. In this way, you can test the spread quickly and efficiently, and everyone involved in the process can weigh in on what they like, what they want to adjust, and how they might use the spread going forward.

4. *Start at the end.* Sometimes, the easiest way to write a tarot spread is to begin at the end or to start by clarifying what you want the final card in your reading to be. Practice writing spreads by starting with the last card in the spread and building forward. If you know that you want your reading to end with advice from the cards, what might you want to explore before reaching that point? What information or observation or truth or insight might be helpful to know in advance?

If you already completed exercise 2, try making a new batch of spreads for those same general prompts using this method. Does this feel easier, more challenging, or about the same? How does it shift your perspective on the function of each position to start at the end?

PART FOUR

REVISING SPREADS

As you get more comfortable with reading spreads, you will start to recognize your own preferences. There may come a time, or you may already be in a moment, when you find a spread that's *close* to what you want—but just isn't quite right. Maybe you have a spread that you use all the time, but it doesn't fit the situation at hand. Or maybe you have a question that's similar to one you've asked before, but you want to come at it from a different angle or incorporate another aspect into the reading.

Maybe you're just bored and want to tweak a spread that you use regularly or haven't used in a while. Maybe you're craving a change, wanting to take control, or are eager to spice something up. Maybe this is just a skill you know will come in handy eventually. I hear you!

So how do we revise a tarot spread to suit our purposes? How do we keep the spread clear and effective while also making necessary adjustments that will help give us the structure and support that we need for our reading? How do we freshen it up or make it more clear, shifting an existing spread into a new direction or energy? Let's talk about it.

What Does It Mean to Revise a Tarot Spread?

Revising a tarot spread is another word for *editing*, *tweaking*, or *adjusting*. Unlike using a tarot spread as it's written or writing a completely new spread from scratch, when we revise a spread, we make a shift or change to an existing spread so that it will better suit our purposes. Just like revising an email, a text, a draft, a song, a recipe, or anything else, this process can happen gradually, all at once, or somewhere in between. But anytime we take a completed, functional spread and make significant changes to it, we are revising that spread.

Sometimes revising a tarot spread is really simple. It might just mean adding another position or two to an existing spread so that we can incorporate another angle, so that we can solicit advice, or so that we can include an insight or perspective that feels important. Other times, revising might be as simple as rewriting one of the positions so that it better suits our particular situation. And still other times, this might involve keeping the base structure of the spread but rewriting all of the positions to get more specific about what we're looking for.

Revising spreads refers to any adjustments that we make to an existing spread, whether it's one that we found in a book, one that we saw online, or one that we wrote ourselves.

Why Would We Revise Existing Tarot Spreads?

Even the most brilliant spread, the most useful spread, the most clear and inspiring spread is not going to work for every imaginable scenario. General spreads can work for any number of situations, and highly specific spreads can help us get deeply granular about what we're looking for. However, if we can't find a spread we want to use, one that will address our particular question or challenge in the way that we need, it requires some extra legwork.

Writing our own spreads, as we discussed earlier, is the ultimate way to craft a fully customized tarot layout that will ensure that we have the kind of conversation that we're looking to have with our cards. But starting from scratch isn't always necessary. Whether you're short on time or just know that a particular flow feels really good for you and would work well for the reading you want to do, knowing how to revise an existing tarot spread is an excellent skill to have in your back pocket.

To give you an example, many relationship spreads include positions that focus on another person's feelings, someone who is not the person pulling cards. And while everyone has their own ethics and morals for reading tarot, one of the lines I personally do not cross is reading into the heart of someone who has not consented to the reading. (It's why I don't do "How do they feel about me?" style relationship readings as part of my professional practice! This isn't to say that these kinds of readings cannot be done ethically; simply that I prefer not to work with tarot in this way.)

But some relationship spreads include really juicy, beautifully crafted prompts around personal reflection, ones that appeal to my own cravings around introspection, awareness, and discovery. So, depending on how the spread is designed, I might be able to either tweak the position I'm not comfortable using, remove it entirely from the spread, or add some prompts in its place that are more in line with my tarot philosophy. In this way, I don't have to start from nothing and build a spread from the ground up. Instead, I can just revise the spread to keep it in line with what I want out of the reading and can more quickly get to pulling cards and addressing my question.

Knowing how to do this, how to thoughtfully tweak existing spreads, can open up many new possibilities for your tarot readings. Rather than having to do research to find the perfect spread written by someone else or to take the time to write a full spread from start to finish, being able to revise an existing spread gives us the confidence to make a spread our own. It means that when you see a new spread in a book or online, you will have the tools you need to make sure that you can use it most effectively for you. And it means that as you continue to develop your own preferences and tastes around tarot spreads, you can adjust any spread to work even better for you.

Remember that tarot spreads are, at their core, suggestions: You can always mix them up to suit you and your questions more accurately.

When Should We *Not* Revise a Tarot Spread?

Knowing how to revise a spread is a clever and useful skill that can take our tarot readings using spreads to the next level. Sometimes, though, revising a spread isn't necessarily the best move or shouldn't be the first thing that we try.

First, if you've already used a spread for a reading and you didn't really get the answer you wanted, don't just adjust the spread a little bit and then reuse it for a new reading on that same topic. You might do this subtly, perhaps without realizing it, or you might be *extremely* aware of what you're doing and decide to follow through anyway. Either way, the cards are likely not going to give you the answer that you're seeking, and they may even call you out on trying to manipulate them or refusing to listen to the insights they are providing. Anytime you approach your tarot cards demanding a specific outcome or only being open to one kind of response, you're already putting yourself in a difficult position. Reading the cards over and over on the same topic, hoping for a different result, is rarely going to work out the way you want it to.

If you do find yourself making minor adjustments to a tarot spread in the hopes that you can immediately use it a second time and get a different outcome on the same exact topic, I will gently instead suggest that you put the cards down and find a different activity. This is a time to take a break and consider the answers that your deck has already provided rather than scrambling to find a different meaning for the cards you've pulled. Grab a journal, call a friend, or go for a walk, but I implore you—don't redo the reading.

I also do not suggest revising a spread when you're halfway through a reading. This might seem like an obvious thing to say, but you'd be surprised; sometimes it's extremely tempting to adjust a spread prompt after pulling a card for it, in the hopes of either not having to work as hard to interpret that card's meaning *or* as a way of helping us get closer to the answer that we might've been looking for.

It's really important to take your time when writing or revising a spread, but it's equally important to be thoughtful and careful when choosing the spread you're actually going to read with. There's really no need to rush the process of selecting your spread and preparing for a reading. Using tarot from a place of urgency is rarely necessary. If you get halfway through a reading, however, and decide that a particular position doesn't fit, it can be really confusing and messy to try to revise that position, especially with any kind of objectivity. If you discover halfway through pulling cards that you're using a spread that doesn't make sense or doesn't apply, I encourage you to put the cards back, consider if you're in the right headspace for reading, and either take a break from the cards for a time or check in with yourself and select a spread that better suits what you're looking for.

Needing to tweak a spread is not unusual, especially if it's one that you've written yourself or one you haven't worked with before. But rewriting the position after you've already pulled the cards, or changing your mind about the spread you want to use halfway through it and trying to just power through without reshuffling and fully starting over, can get messy. Tarot readings, especially around sensitive topics or really personal subjects, can already put us into a vulnerable space. Don't make it more complicated for yourself.

The last thing I'll add here is something that may feel a bit vague but that I still want to include: If your intuition is telling you that a particular spread doesn't fit, or if you feel discomfort around using a certain spread, listen to that impulse. Even if you can't find anything practically wrong with the spread, even if you feel as though you've adjusted a spread well and it suits your purposes, if there's something in you that says it's not quite right, *let yourself listen*. Learning to trust your intuition in tarot, inside and outside of readings, is a powerful practice. Don't discount any misgivings you may feel, even if you can't quite articulate where those misgivings may be coming from.

What Skills Do We Need to Revise a Spread?

This book covers three separate topics around tarot spreads: reading spreads, writing spreads, and revising spreads. There's also an important reason that this part of the book is placed after the sections on reading and writing tarot spreads: because being proficient in both using *and* creating spreads is an essential skill for revising existing spreads effectively. Revising might seem easier than writing spreads from scratch (and it can be!), but it requires finesse, experience, and insight to know which string to pull on in a fully finished spread in order to have the desired result.

I don't say this just to gatekeep what might seem like the quickest way to create an original spread. I promise I'm not trying to make this an elite skill that's only for pros! It's simply that knowing how to read a tarot spread well and understanding what it takes to create a spread from scratch help you understand how a spread functionally works. Plus, both skills come in handy when you're assessing and adjusting an existing spread. The more you know about your own reading preferences and your own favorite spread prompts, as well as about how you like to craft your own spreads, the easier it will be to revise an existing spread quickly, efficiently, and effectively. But like everything with tarot, doing so takes practice. And practice, in this case, comes from reading with and writing spreads.

You don't necessarily need to be writing brand new tarot spreads every day to start utilizing revision skills. However, I recommend in general that you start with revising spreads that you have already used in readings, ideally ones that you've used more than once. For many people, revising an existing spread is a more straightforward process than writing a completely new one, but this process becomes even easier when it's a spread that you're comfortable with, one that you already understand.

The more we are familiar with a particular spread, the more we know how to use it as the blueprint for our readings, and the easier it becomes to tweak and adjust it. The spread becomes a familiar tool, one that we begin to know intimately. And in working with that base spread multiple times, we may be able to revisit it and continue tweaking it as needed.

Consider the alternative: If you aren't sure what kinds of spread prompts really work for you, if an existing tarot spread feels strange or confusing, then adjusting it might not really add much value to that spread as a tool. You're working entirely in the realm of the theoretical. Again, that approach might suit you. If you're someone who is extremely comfortable reading spreads in general, it might be easy for you to take a spread apart mentally and piece it together in a new way without having to use that spread in readings. In general, though, I recommend beginning by revising spreads you already know.

How Do We Revise a Spread?

The first step in revising an existing spread is in studying and understanding the spread as written. Beyond clarifying what the purpose of the spread is, what its function is, what kind of theme and topic it's investigating, and the other content of the spread itself, it's also important to understand the structure of the spread so that we know how our changes will impact the overall flow.

First, acknowledge *why* the spread was originally written. How does it function? What question is this spread answering, and how does it approach that question? What topic is it tackling, and what angle is it coming at this topic from? What about the spread really works for your particular question, and what perhaps doesn't work as well?

Look thoughtfully at each position in the original spread. How many cards are in the spread? What purpose does each position serve? How does each position set up the next one? What story does the spread tell?

Consider the first card in the spread. How does this card set the tone for the spread itself? Where does it anchor you in the reading? How does it introduce the topic at hand and pave the way for all of the cards that follow? Pay attention as well to the final card in the spread. Where will this card leave you? What does it offer as a final piece of advice or support, encouragement, or truth? Does the spread end with a call to action, or is it more about internal exploration, discovery, awareness, insight, or perception? Does this spread invite you to keep reflecting when the reading is done, or does it instead give you something tangible to do? And lastly, look at the cards that connect the beginning and the end of the spread. What is being explored? How does the reading progress? What information or truths are uncovered and explored? What gets left out of the conversation?

Now take a moment to reflect on what about the spread doesn't feel like it works for you. Or to say another way: Specifically which parts of the spread do you think you would like to change or revise? The answer might be really easy to nail down because it might be as simple as one specific position not working or your need to add a card or two to the overall layout. Sometimes just creating some more specificity in a spread is all that's needed to make it more applicable for your desired reading. Other times, you might just want to remove a single position in order to make the spread function more comfortable for you.

If you can't immediately pinpoint what about the spread doesn't suit, or if it seems as though every position might require tweaking, that might take a little bit more time to unpack. Pay attention to words that don't feel quite right, or individual prompts that may approach the situation from an angle that doesn't resonate. This step is really about identifying the aspects you want to change and honing in on what you want to revise.

> Note: If you feel the need to adjust every position significantly, you may be better served by writing your own spread or by doing a bit more research to find a base spread that's more appropriate for your question. If nothing about the spread really works for you, you might be making more work for yourself than necessary by trying to revise it.

If there's a specific card position that you want to adjust, and you've decided to move forward with revising this spread, consider first what that particular card accomplishes functionally within the spread. What does it do? What does it offer? What role does it serve? Does changing this prompt disrupt the functionality or flow of the entire spread? Sometimes the easiest way to figure that out is to consider how the reading would work if that position were completely removed and not replaced with anything else. Does the spread still make sense? Does it still work as is?

Once you understand how each card position fits into the overall structure, you can make your revisions with more care. It might be that after adjusting this position, you also need to tweak another position or two, to ensure that they're still necessary and functional within the spread. The last thing you want to do is revise the spread in a way that means it doesn't ultimately work!

There are a few different ways to revise, edit, or alter an existing spread, each of which I'll explore here. And if only one card position is really the sticking point, by doing this prep work around examining the spread as is, you can move ahead with one (or several!) of the following steps to customize your spread for a more personalized experience.

When trying out these techniques, move slowly, and take things one step at a time. This process doesn't have to take hours and hours, but it does require some care. I highly recommend working card by card, rather than trying to adjust multiple positions simultaneously. Each card has its own impact on the reading, so sometimes just adjusting a single prompt can have a big ripple effect on how the spread functions. Don't rush this process or try to do too much at once. Let this be a playful experiment, a skill you are working to build rather than something you expect to immediately nail on the first try. Remember too that sometimes a spread that you initially think will need a lot of changes will actually serve its purpose with just a small tweak or two, while other times a position that you thought would work just fine without edits may eventually need to be rewritten.

Adding a Card Position

Adding a card without changing any of the existing positions is often the easiest way to customize a spread for your own purposes. This choice is particularly useful if you're looking for insights or advice, if you want to personalize an existing spread for a very specific function, or if you'd like to try to see a silver lining in a difficult situation. These types of card positions can often be added into the beginning, middle, or ending of an existing spread without really disrupting what's already happening. If you're in a situation where a written spread already provides a lot of necessary insights and truths, but you have a specific ask for the cards in addition to what is already being explored, adding in a simple position or two to address that can often be easier than just starting from scratch and writing a completely new spread.

Just like when you're writing a spread from scratch, revisions can provide a great opportunity for reflection or journaling before you try to put a spread together. Taking a moment to pause and consider what you really crave from the cards can make all the difference in the building of the spread itself, and writing down those thoughts can help you distill those truths into spread positions. What kinds of information, support, advice, insights, truths, perspectives, or tangible action items are you hoping to receive from the cards? What emotion are you hoping to feel when the tarot reading is complete? What guidance or advice do you want to walk away from the reading with?

Now, don't misunderstand me here: You may know what you hope to receive from a spread, and not actually receive it during your reading. But being disappointed by your reading is not necessarily a reflection of the spread itself—it may simply be a reaction to the content of the reading. Sometimes we're really hoping for comfort from a tarot reading, but the cards may have some hard truths for us to acknowledge instead. But if the spread itself doesn't leave space for the kinds of information or encouragement that you're really hoping for, it's unlikely that the reading will leave you feeling as though your question was fully answered. Not liking the answer is not the same thing as not asking the right questions, but in creating an original or revised spread, it's essential that we create the space for the *kinds* of answers we are looking for.

An example of this might be someone wanting to do a reading around their relationship with money. There are a lot of spreads about money in the world, but money is a really personal thing, and different people have different hangups or challenges or struggles that they often hope to address with the cards around this topic. Perhaps after doing research and taking some time for introspection, this person finds a spread that comes close to what they're looking for: general positions around money, hangups, and money trauma, as well as prompts for how to move through that trauma or how to hold space for these challenges.

This person might see enough of what they look to explore with the tarot in this spread to want to move forward with it. We're going to use this spread as the basis for our revision exercises, so for the purposes of simplicity, we'll call this the Original Money Spread:

The Original Money Spread

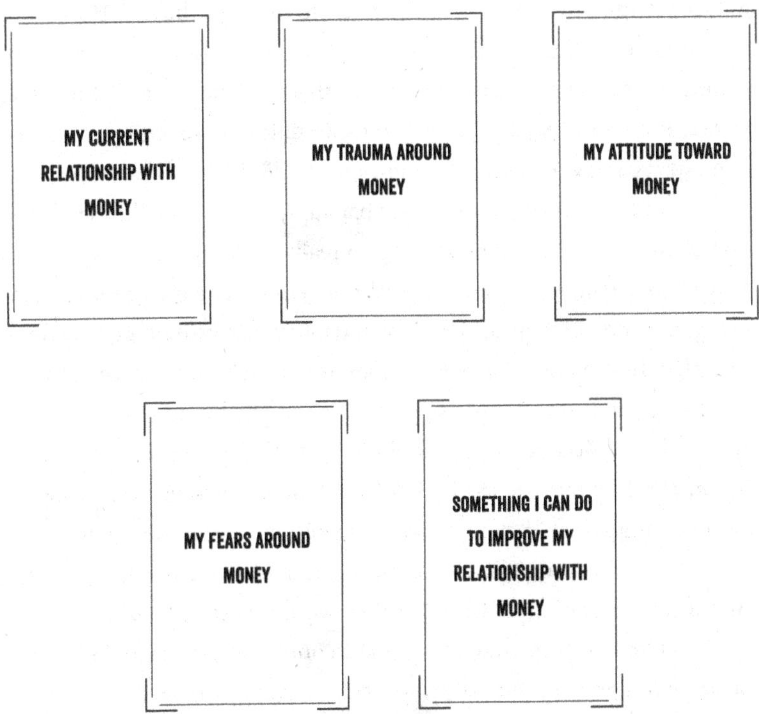

my current relationship with money / my trauma around money / my attitude toward money / my fears around money / something I can do to improve my relationship with money

This sample money spread is mainly built of positions exploring the present moment: the querent's present relationship with money, as well as the current attitude or mindset, and current fears that may be manifesting in specific ways. The position for trauma makes space for past events, experiences, or emotions around money, digging into any foundational issues or sources that have contributed to the present moment. The final position allows the cards to offer some practical advice for something the querent can do to improve the situation.

In general, this spread covers a lot of bases and may be close to suiting the querent's needs. But let's say that this querent is feeling very tender about money and their relationship to it. Perhaps this person has been struggling with a scarcity mindset, and while they want to be realistic about their money traumas and hangups, they also could use a little boost. This reader might be looking to really build up their confidence around managing their own money, budgeting their own money, and being in control of their own money, and might also be looking for assurance that they're not as bad with money as they believe themselves to be.

Now, given the sample spread, there might be different ways to approach this situation. They could just use the spread as written and be on the lookout for cards that offer encouragement and insights around things that they're good at. In other words, they could just hope to receive some positive reinforcement by using the spread as is. But, if they wanted to ensure that they would receive the kind of support they're really craving, this person could also go ahead and add a position designed specifically to provide some additional bolstering or encouragement. If you like, take a moment to brainstorm some potential prompts that could suit this need.

Again, there are plenty of ways to do this and many potential positions that could be added. Below is just one example of the original money spread, revised to **add** an additional position for encouragement.

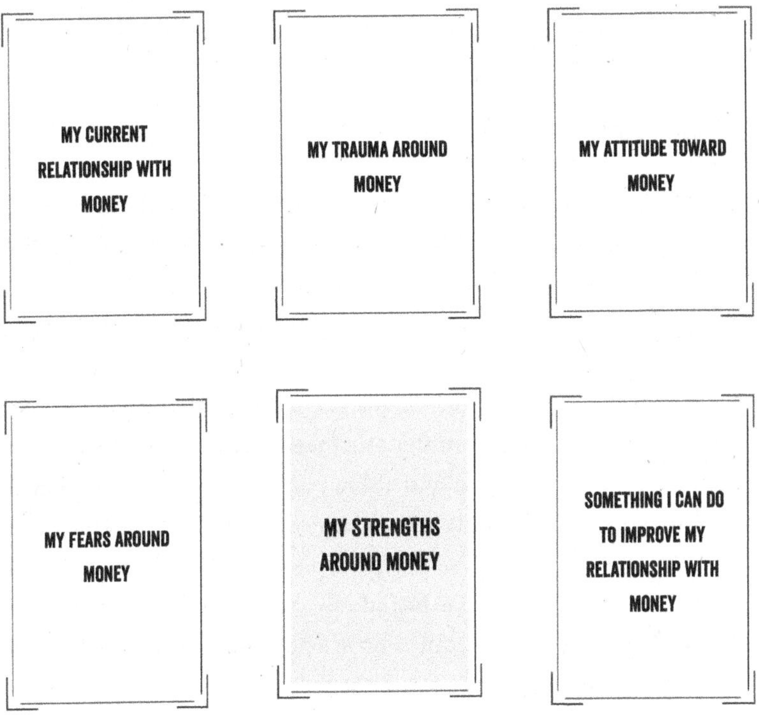

my current relationship with money / my trauma around money / my attitude toward money / my fears around money / ***my strengths around money*** */ something I can do to improve my relationship with money*

In this adjusted sample money spread, you can see that the overall theme of the spread—and the resulting reading that might come out of it—hasn't necessarily changed a lot: This is still a spread about money. But when an additional position is added, this reading can ensure that the querent in this case will get the gentle support that they are really craving and receive knowledge around some positive strengths that they may already possess on this topic in addition to the other insights provided through the reading.

Removing a Card Position

Like adding a card position to a spread, removing a card can be fairly simple on the surface. But taking a card away, while it may simplify the overall reading by shortening it, can have a big impact on what the spread focuses on, and it requires a little more care than adding a position might.

Personally, I find this technique the most helpful when a spread feels as though it includes positions that seem redundant or if a position takes the spread in a direction that I'm not interested in going. Sometimes longer spreads may dig into an angle that isn't very relevant to the ultimate question or may include prompts that feel similar enough to me that I don't see the need to include all of them. Since I tend to prefer shorter spreads anyway, if I can remove a position to get to the heart of my question more concisely, I will usually do so!

Remember our money spread example from earlier? Let's revisit the initial spread and consider removing a position rather than adding one to see how it impacts the overall flow of the reading.

The Original Money Spread:

my current relationship with money / my trauma around money / my attitude toward money / my fears around money / something I can do to improve my relationship with money

Perhaps the same reader from earlier wants to reuse this spread, since it worked well for them when they were in a tender place around money. But perhaps during that reading, the money trauma position brought up something really real, and they're not particularly interested in digging into that again right now. This reader might want to remove that position from the spread and see how it impacts the reading, focusing more on the present and potential future rather than dwelling too much on the past. If you like, take a moment to brainstorm what this spread would look like if you removed various prompts.

In this adjusted sample money spread, the spread still functions but is a bit more concise. When we **remove** the trauma-focused position, this spread gets a bit lighter, while still holding space for fears or existing attitudes, and continuing to offer some guidance on ways to improve challenging aspects around money. The reader can now test this spread with the knowledge that they are protecting themselves and focusing on what they can control, rather than looking backward at something that they may not want to wrestle with in this specific reading.

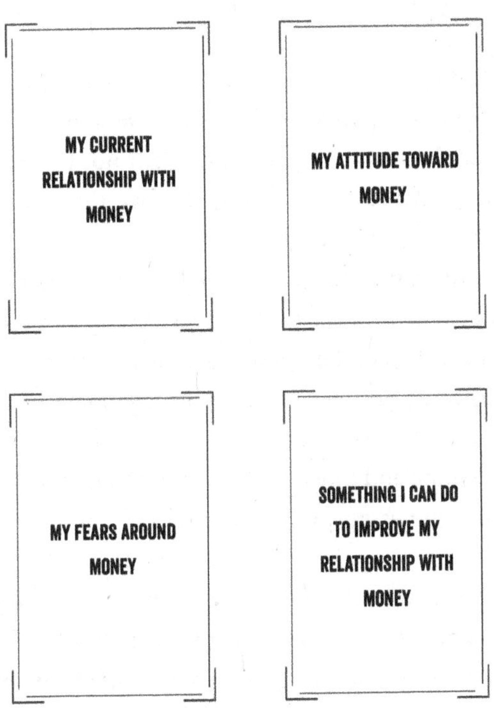

my current relationship with money / ~~my trauma around money~~ / my attitude toward money / my fears around money / something I can do to improve my relationship with money

Editing a Card Position

Sometimes adding or removing a card position isn't quite enough to make the spread as impactful or focused as we want it to be. In these cases, the exact language of a position might not be precise or clear enough, or a particular position might move the reading toward a specific direction that isn't needed or wanted.

Editing card positions allows for nearly endless possibilities around customization. Sometimes just changing a word or two can impact the entire vibe of the spread, shifting the focus in a useful way. In my experience, editing card positions can have the biggest impact with the least amount of effort—but like adding and removing a prompt, needs to be done with intention and care in order to get the clearest result.

Let's revisit our sample money spread and our hypothetical tarot reader again.

Perhaps our dear reader, who has used this spread a few times now in different moments, has realized that they do like having a position that addresses money traumas or challenges around money that might be getting in their way. But maybe the phrase *money trauma* in the original money spread feels activating, stressful, or too heavy for what they're looking for. Maybe they don't consider their history or personal past with money traumatic: *Trauma* can be a big word and might just feel like too much for the reading they want to do.

The Original Money Spread:

my current relationship with money / my trauma around money / my attitude toward money / my fears around money / something I can do to improve my relationship with money

Instead of removing the trauma position entirely, let's edit it. If you like, take a moment to test out some rewrites for the trauma-themed prompt.

____

____

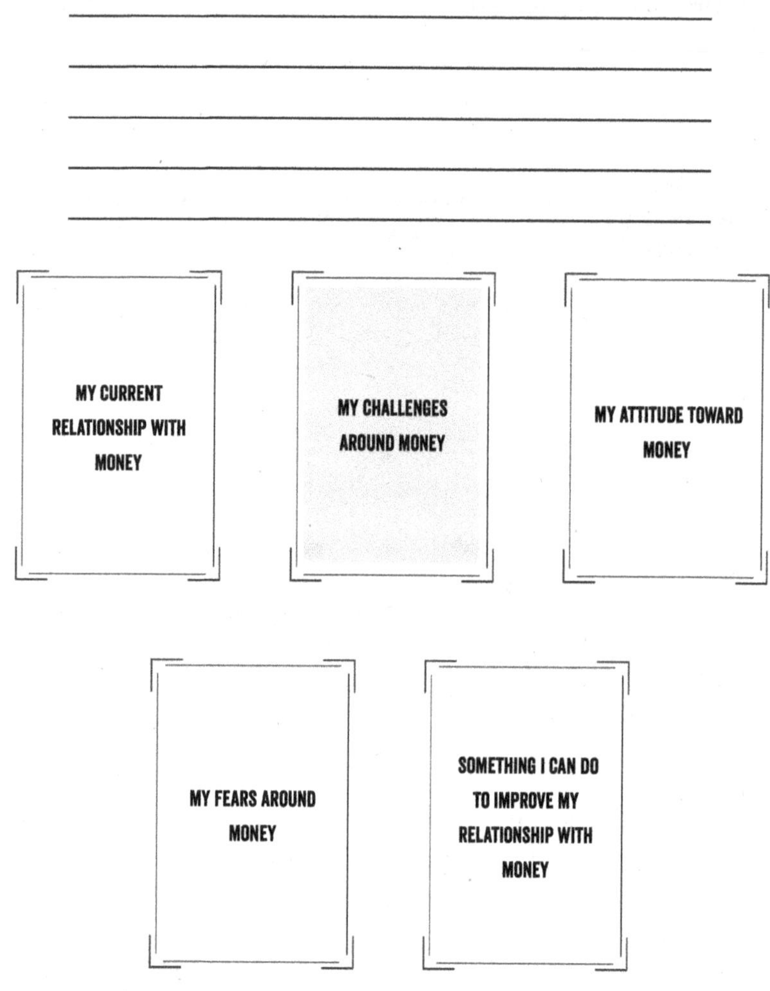

my current relationship with money / ***my challenges around money*** */ my attitude toward money / my fears around money / something I can do to improve my relationship with money*

When we **reword** the trauma position into a gentler and more relevant phrase, focusing on words like *discomfort* or *challenges*, this spread stays grounded in the present but digs deeper into what may be serving as an obstacle, difficulty, or frustration when it comes to dealing with finances. This edit may better suit the reader's history, personality, or needs for the reading better than the original money spread as written, without making the reading unnecessarily activating.

The overall flow of the spread has not changed, but the impact that this may have on the querent is significant.

Making Multiple Adjustments

Of course, all of these things may be true at once! It could be that one position needs to be removed; adding another position might improve the general flow; and editing a position or two could provide precisely the clarity, support, and insight that the querent is looking for.

Often, revising a spread takes a few efforts. I often find that it's helpful to move through a few different ways of editing before choosing the final version. Spreads are naturally flexible containers: Making multiple adjustments might be necessary to create the specific boundaries that we need to guide the reading. If you think that your spread might need multiple adjustments, try doing them one at a time, moving slowly and deliberately.

Let's return to our original sample money spread and our sample reader one final time.

Perhaps after playing around with each of these different versions of the spread, the reader realizes that while the backbone of the spread is really strong, a few tweaks in various spots really make it feel like a spread they can use over and over again. They like the various edits that they've made for various needs but are now looking to turn this spread into something they can use again and again, a tool that they can reach for whenever they're feeling active or stressed or uncertain around money.

This reader may begin with the version of the spread that includes a strength position, wanting to ensure that there's some encouragement and gentle support around money. They may also have found that they really prefer the adjustment in the money trauma position, and they like keeping this spread grounded in the present. Having used the spread a few times in a few different ways now, perhaps this querent has realized that they have some other unaddressed emotions around money and want to make sure that there's room to explore that in the moments when big feelings are bubbling up. This may inspire them to create an additional prompt that makes space for hopes or fears around money.

Combining their skills of spread revision with their own lived experience in using this spread, this querent may ultimately come up with a revised spread that looks like this:

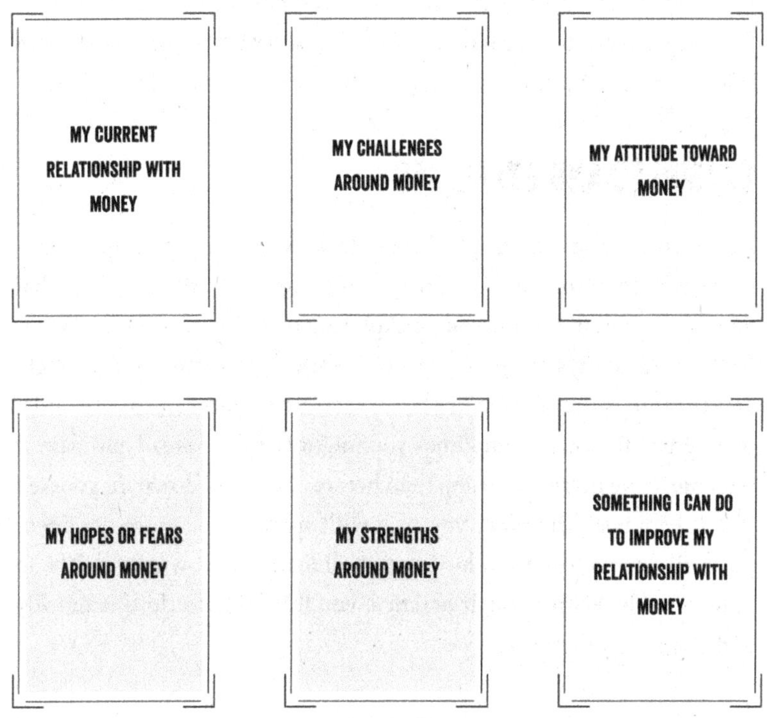

my current relationship with money / my challenges around money / my attitude toward money / ***my hopes or fears*** *around money /* ***my strengths around money*** */ something I can do to improve my relationship with money*

When we adjust one individual position to better reflect the mindset and needs of the reader, and add in additional positions that provide the kind of support that this reader is craving, the resulting spread has a pretty different vibe from the original. It's certainly still about money, and even includes space for both challenges and hopes around money topics. But now the reader knows very well how this spread functions for them and can reach for this tool for a wide variety of situations, with full awareness of what this spread has to offer them as an individual.

EXAMPLES AND EXERCISES

Just as in writing fully original spreads from scratch, revising spreads gets easier the more you practice. I have a few different exercises that you can try out in order to begin exploring how this process might feel for you. As always, remember to go slowly, be patient with yourself, and try things out. Play is key here: revising requires flexibility and a willingness to fail, as sometimes you might tweak a spread and have it turn out to be more confusing than before. Don't get down on yourself if that happens! The more you play with spreads, the more confident you will become, and the more you will learn about what you like in your spreads. With enough practice, you'll be able to do this quickly and almost instinctively.

1. Add a position. Let's start by just adding a prompt to a simple, general spread that you're already probably familiar with. The *past / present / future* spread is a three-card classic and is one that can be used in any number of situations around endless topics. This spread is written in such a way that we can hold a truth or question in our minds while using the spread and get a great result. And while this spread can work really well in a general way, I tend to find it most useful when thinking about a particular aspect of life, or a particular thread that extends from past to future. Using this general spread as a baseline and adding specificity into it can make it more relatable and easier to use around particular questions.

Let's experiment with making the spread more specific for a few different topics. What would it look like to examine the past, present, and future of various aspects of self, community, career, love, family, creativity, aspirations, fears, or another topic? Where could you add a single position in a way that impacts the entire spread and adds specificity as needed?

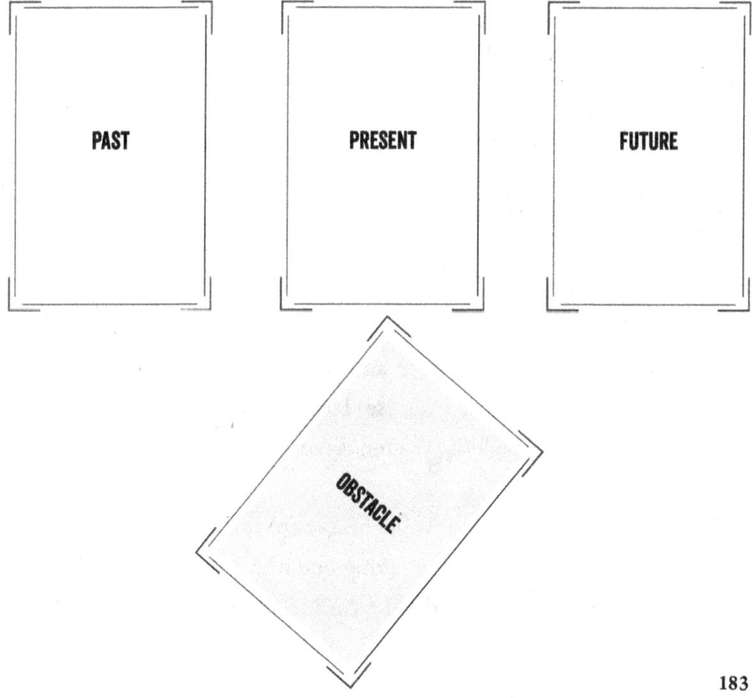

Practice adding a position at the beginning, middle, and end of the spread, and test each version. How does adding the card in different areas of the spread impact the final reading? Does it feel most comfortable for you to add a prompt to one part of the spread over another?

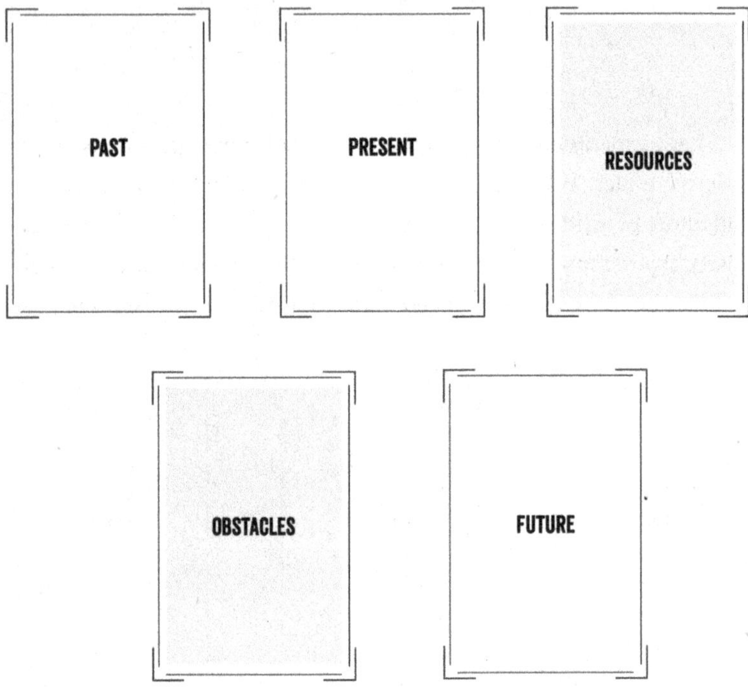

If you like, add a position to another spread that you work with often, and follow this same exercise. How does adding an additional card to the reading impact the overall direction, flow, and result?

2. *Remove a position.* Let's repeat the first exercise, but instead of adding a position to the spread, let's try taking one out. Start with one of your practice spreads, where you added a card to the *past / present / future*

general spread, and try removing one of the positions—but not the one that you added. Play around with different versions of this spread, and see how it impacts the reading to fully remove one of these positions.

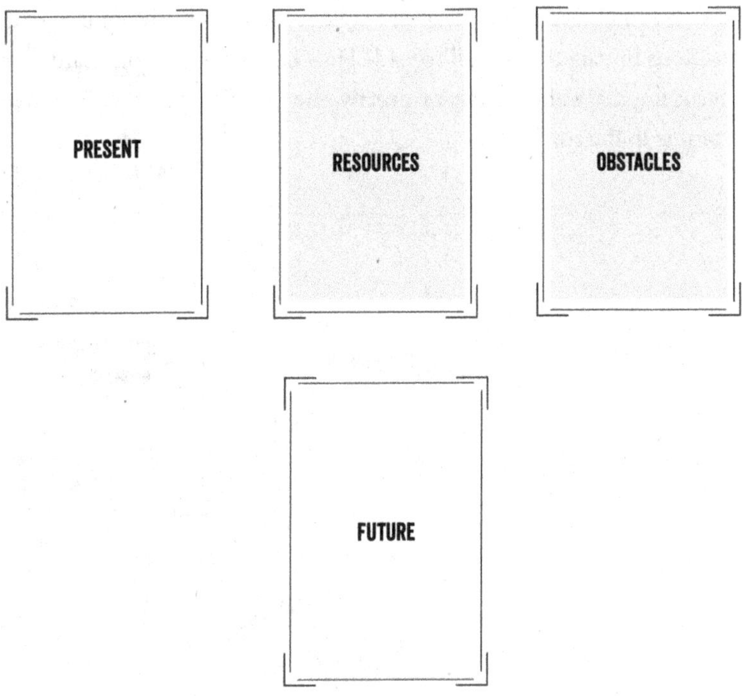

Repeat this exercise with any additional practice spread that you've made or with another general spread that you use all the time. What changes? How does removing a card change the flow of the reading? Which cards can you reasonably remove, and which ones feel essential to maintain the flow and impact of the reading?

3. *Edit a position.* By now you can probably see where we're going: It's time to edit a position. Again, I recommend playing around with one of your four-card practice spreads from the *past / present / future* experiment and editing a position to help it better serve the overall flow and intention of the desired reading. How does editing different positions impact the overall spread? How can you tweak one card and have it impact, either subtly or overtly, the meaning of all of the other prompts in the spread?

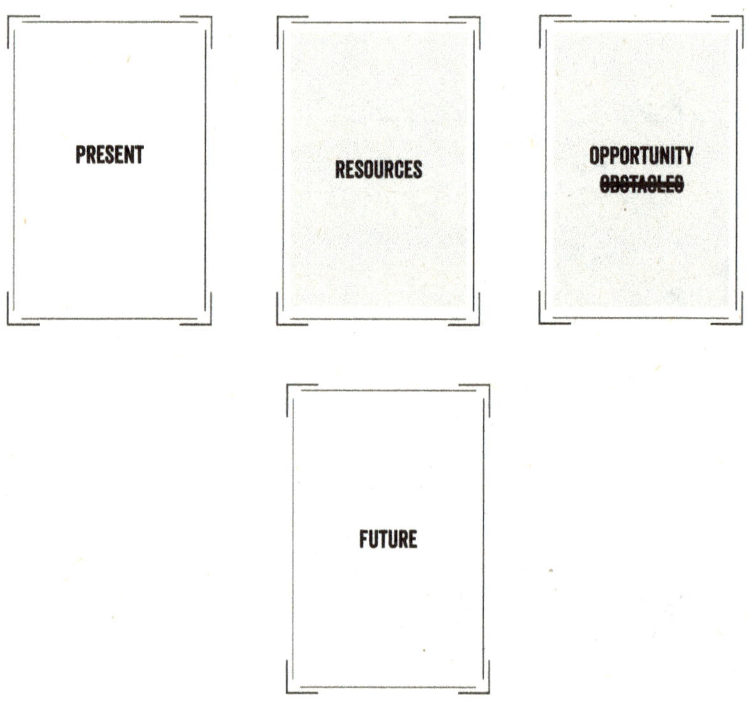

Try this with a spread you use all the time, one that you know well. Go through each position and edit it, one at a time, leaving the other positions the same. How do these small shifts change the flow of the reading? How big a change can you make by editing only one position?

4. *Make multiple adjustments.* When you're comfortable playing around with single changes in a spread, try making a few adjustments to one spread. This isn't always necessary, but it's worth practicing. Doing this can also help you see just how easy it is to have a huge impact on a spread's overall flow and outcome by revising rather than fully writing something new.

You can do this a few different ways: first, by continuing to edit a spread that you already worked with, or by starting from scratch and making multiple revisions on an existing spread that you haven't played with yet. I recommend practicing by doing both! As demonstrated in the earlier money spread example, often multiple adjustments happen over time, as you revisit a spread and tweak it for each specific reading. But the more you get comfortable with these techniques, the more empowered you may feel to adjust spreads as needed to suit your specific needs or to personalize published spreads in order to ensure that they will help you explore your questions.

PART FIVE

SPREADS FOR EVERY OCCASION

What you'll find in this section is a large assortment of tarot spreads for you to explore, consider, play with, and use. While you are absolutely encouraged to use them as is and as written, they can also serve as a starting point for you, regardless of how simple or complex they may be. Adjust them as needed, adding or subtracting positions, tweaking words, or rewriting aspects that don't work for you or that you want to be more specific. And if none of the spreads quite suit, you can also use these as jumping-off points for creating entirely new spreads. If a spread inspires you to use its framework in a new way, go for it.

Even the most polished and powerful spread isn't necessarily going to serve every person, all of the time. This spreads library is an opportunity for you to find what you need, and if you don't see it, to use the various skills and techniques we've explored in other parts of the book to ensure that you can tailor a tarot spread just for you. Pay attention to the spreads that you like, that you feel drawn to, as well as any that don't quite work for you. If you find one that you keep returning to, add it to your personal tarot grimoire, and incorporate it into your regular tarot reading routines. And if you like, play with adjusting it to suit more specific circumstances, different questions, or another topic. Truly, the sky's the limit.

These spreads are a blend of classic spreads that you may see in other tarot books and spreads that I have created. Some may feel familiar, whereas others are brand new for this collection. I encourage you to skim all of the spreads here, to mark any that you may want to return to or that you might want to try editing, revising, or tweaking. If you're looking for a spread around a specific topic, you will likely find it here, but you still might find value in exploring the entire collection because sometimes subjects overlap or a spread could suit a number of situations.

In addition to the spreads I share in this book, I've also written hundreds and hundreds of other tarot spreads over the years of my professional career. For even more spreads, I highly encourage you to check out my website: *www.3amtarot.com*. Here you'll find an archive of even more original tarot spreads broken into topics and themes, along with links to my writing, courses, and other tarot resources.

The Classics

Please note that many of these spreads are written as questions or prompts directed toward a general "you." The "you" in question could be you—the reader and querent—but could also be the querent if you find yourself using these spreads to read for others. Other spreads are written with a more personal "I." Feel free to adjust the language accordingly as needed.

Single-Card Readings

General questions:

What do I need to know today?

What do I need to hear today?

What should I pay attention to today?

What advice do you have for me today?

How can I take care of myself today?

What do I need to know about ____ today?

What's something I need to keep in mind today?

What's an intention I should set for today?

How can I be patient / kind / courageous / generous / empowered / badass / etc. today?

What's something I should remember today?

What's something I should release today?

Why am I feeling anxious / confused / discouraged / indecisive / etc. today?

What intention should I set for today?

Two-Card Cross

General prompts:

situation / challenge

desire / obstacle

hope / fear

reality / perception

above / below

pro / con

what's clear / what's confusing

something you know / something you don't know

what you believe / what you know

want / need

Three-Card Reading

Basic prompts:

body / mind / spirit

past / present / future

situation / advice / potential outcome

strength / weakness / growth

opportunity / obstacle / potential outcome

stop / start / continue

you / your current path / your current potential

goals / obstacles / resources

release / receive / retain

desire / conflict / resolution

situation / lesson / advice

Celtic Cross:

Because this spread is so commonly used and shared, I'm including it here in the classics section. This ten-card spread is incredibly popular and deeply beloved by those who use it. But I do not consider it a particularly beginner-friendly spread, given its length and complexity. If you're just getting started in a tarot practice, I recommend getting comfortable with two- or three-card spreads first. If you are just dying to try it regardless of its length, try using it for a general reading rather than digging into a specific question. You may find it easier to get familiar with the positions when the stakes don't feel quite as high!

Please also note that while the Celtic Cross spread was first published in 1910, its origins are unknown, and thus, there are many, many different versions of this spread out in the world. Everyone reads it a bit differently! The following positions are merely suggestions, based on my own spread preferences and the generous knowledge of Mary K. Greer, Carrie Mallon, Beth Maiden, and other tarot writers whose work I admire. Feel free to adjust accordingly.

The layout is shown on page 196.

10
5
9
4
1
6
2
8
3
7

Card one: *broad themes, your present moment, where things currently stand*

Card two: *present obstacles, challenges, imbalances, or other relevant information*

Card three: *how you got here, foundations of situation, unconscious or subconscious influences*

Card four: *the recent past, an energy that is receding or releasing, something behind you*

Card five: *possibilities, goals, longings, where you hope to go, conscious desires or ambitions*

Card six: *a way the situation may develop, your ability to take action, something before you*

Card seven: *your current attitude, your power in the situation, a way you see yourself*

Card eight: *your current environment, the way others perceive or impact you, influences and factors*

Card nine: *your hopes or fears, shadow work, a lesson to learn, your outlook or perspective*

Card ten: *longer-term outcome of this path if nothing changes, culmination, advice*

Interrogation Spreads

Deck interview spread:

this deck's personality / this deck's strengths / this deck's limits / moments we should work together or topics that this deck is uniquely suited to explore / potential challenges to note / something beautiful that this deck can teach me

What kind of tarot reader are you?

my general vibe as a reader / my strengths as a reader / my limits or growth areas as a reader / a way that I am unique / a talent or skill to incorporate into my tarot work / something that I can work on

you as a tarot reader / why clients choose you / your strengths as a reader / resources that may help you / how to develop deeper skills / potential for your future as a reader

Understanding a particular card:

how is this card relevant to my present? / what could this card teach me? / how could this card challenge me?

a reason that this card is important for me right now / something that is preventing me from hearing this card's message / a way to release any blockages

Spreads for Specific Themes

These spreads generally have three to five cards; any more than that can tend to confuse, complicate, and cloud the outcome.

Transitions and Making Decisions

option one / option two / advice

something that is stagnant / something that is moving / something you can do

the best that could happen / the worst that could happen / what I actually want to do

where you are / where you want to go / how to bridge the gap

something positive a yes could bring / something unexpected a yes could introduce / something else

a truth to explore / a risk to consider / an insight to acknowledge / a fear to honor / a next step

a fear that is holding you back / a strength or talent you possess / a good thing that could emerge

an insight into your goal / an obstacle / a potential success / a detail to attend to / a next step

something to do / something not to do / something else to know

red light: stop or pause / green light: all systems go / yellow light: slow down and use caution

you, right now / a change you fear / a dream you cherish / a success you crave / your desired future

an insight into your current state / a reminder of your power / something you can do right now

where ya going? / whatcha doing? / whatcha looking for?

a point of friction / a need for change / an old belief to release

something that is shifting / something that is staying the same / something that needs to grow

action / stagnation / tension / release

a way to slow down / a way to hold space / a way to feel your feelings

an old restriction to challenge / a new framework to explore / an important question to ask / an open door to walk through

a truth that is breaking through / a new way to examine that truth / an insight that you haven't yet considered / a first step that you can take right now

Reflection and Self-Awareness

something you love / something you need / something you are being offered

a doubt to hold space for / a gift you already possess / an insight at your fingertips something to recognize / something to surrender / a revelation

a real fear / a true fact / a kind word

something you know / something you are discovering / something you can't see clearly yet

how I feel / what I think / what I'm longing for / something I need

a lesson from the past to lean on / something important in my present / a joy in my future

a heavy emotion / a gentle longing / an action I can take

what feels good? / what feels confusing? / what have I learned? / what's next?

how you feel right now / an underlying need / a worry that's holding you back / something to help

what is my magic? / how does my magic manifest? / what does my magic need? / how can I use my magic to its fullest potential?

a way that you shine / a beauty you possess but overlook / a way that others see you

the brilliance in my fire / the wisdom in my air / the grace in my water / the power in my earth / the beauty in my spirit

something you're ignoring / how to acknowledge it / what to do next

Relationships and Community

For partners and friendships:

you / the other person / an insight into your connection

an insight into my relationship / something to know about me / something to know about the other person / something that connects us / an issue to attend to / a way to strengthen our connection

something you both want / something you both need / something to explore together

a way that your love manifests / a way that their love manifests / a language you speak together

For community of all kinds:

my relationship with creativity / my perspective on community / a way that these can intersect

a value you hold dear / an insight into your emotions / a step toward finding community

something to collectively acknowledge / something to collectively adjust / something to collectively anticipate

the vibe of the community you crave / a way to build it

a fear you carry / a truth to remember / a way to build new relationships / a way to protect existing relationships

For disagreements, conflicts, and misunderstandings:

your perspective / their perspective / root of the conflict or disagreement

something to acknowledge to yourself / something to express to someone else / something to remember while communicating / a way to make amends / a lesson for next time

the heart of your mistake / a way to repair the damage

what you need to heal / what you can do for yourself / what you need from someone else

Desire

what do I want? / why do I want it? / what need might it satisfy?

a desire / a need / a place they intersect

a longing that is being suppressed / something it's manifesting as / something you can do

truth / dare

something you think you want / something you actually want

a path that is opening / a dream that is distracting / something to honor within yourself

a desire that scares you / what that fear actually is / a way to move forward

Creativity

a theme for your project / something to remember / something to release / a way to maintain balance / a goal to focus on

a topic or theme to explore / a medium or method to play with / a support system to consider

something that is working / something to revise or reconsider / something to try out

your vision / your voice / your resources

where is your imagination expanding? / what desire or dream wants to be explored? / where does your creativity live?

inspiration / power / magic

a place to find motivation and energy / a way to stay focused and inspired / a reminder of your magic and strength

an obstacle to examine / a way to show yourself grace / a prompt to explore / something new to try

Career

something I'm good at / something I enjoy / something that encompasses both

something you're curious about / something you keep returning to / an aspect of yourself to take pride and joy in / a way to explore these things further a way this job suits me / a way this job does not suit me / a way to bridge the gap

path one / path two / path three / additional insight

a job for now / a job to aspire to / a job to avoid

be slow / go harder

get focused / loosen up

something you have / something you crave / something you are becoming

something you're good at / something you love to do / something you don't mind doing for money

a way that you're brave / a way to be patient / a legacy you're creating

Money

my relationship with money / where it's been / where it's going

my money past / my money present / my money challenges / my money solutions

a fear around money / a truth around money / something to remember when you're stressed

a money area to get under control / a money area to loosen up around less of this / more of this

spending / saving / savoring

what my finances need / something I can do to get there

money anxiety / money freedom / money power

Activism

a skill or resource you possess / a way to support those existing skills / an activism role you can fill right now / something else you need to know

an action you've been taking / an effect it's having on you / an effect it's having on others

your courage / your conviction

something you're willing to fight for / something you're willing to surrender

something unique you have to offer / a way that your vision is powerful / a way to care for yourself

an area you are gifted in / something to remember / something to consider next

a strength you have / a resource to utilize / a truth to hold fast to

a healing gift you possess / an impact you have / a personal support ritual to implement a big picture truth to remember / a way to stay organized / an important reminder

a way to stay safe / a way to be bold / an impact you're already having

a story you need to tell / a truth you need to amplify / a message you need to explore

something others look to you for / wisdom that others need to hear / a way to tend your own heart

something you believe / something you stand for / something to be proud of

something you're good at / an internal hangup to address / a way to use your skills

listen up / speak up

Hard Times

a root of your anger / something you need to hear / something you need to do

to calm your mind / to soothe your heart / to rest your body

what's going on? / what can I do about it?

a buried emotion / a truth at the core of your numbness or avoidance / something you can do to feel again

a root of your fear / a form your courage takes / something good to look to

an internal blockage to notice / a tender feeling to protect / a way to hold on to your empathy

what are you afraid of? / what can you do about it?

what is blocking your hope? / how can you find it again?

the root of your feelings / an internal narrative to release / an external action to take

a mistake to acknowledge / something it's taught you / a lesson to carry forward

what am I afraid of? / why am I getting lost in this fear? / what's something I can do to feel powerful?

Health and Healing

where to focus healing / how to recover / what to remember / what to release

a truth to recognize / a limit to honor / a way to care for yourself

something you can control / something you cannot control / something to embrace

where does your power live? / how can you use it?

a place to be tender / a place to challenge yourself / a way to balance the two how you're feeling right now / how your community is feeling right now / something you can offer / something you can ask for

something you've had too much of / a reason you may have overindulged / something to soothe your head and heart

something to forgive yourself for / how to be kind to yourself / a way to ground

Daily Life

morning / afternoon / evening

overall theme of the day / something to pay attention to / advice to remember

overall theme of the day / a challenge to reflect on / a lesson to carry forward

something to watch for / something to listen for / something to wait for

something to do / something to say / something to feel

an opportunity / a challenge / advice for the day

pick it up / put it down

an insight into your current state / a reminder of your power / something you can do right now

Future

something to know / something to anticipate / something to discover

next week / next month / next year

Q1 / Q2 / Q3 / Q4

a lesson from the past / a joy in the present / a gift in the future

something you already know is on the way / something to stop worrying about

a way that you will shine / a magic you are building / a gift that is on its way

a future fear to acknowledge / a way it is holding you back in the present / something you can do

Celebration

General celebration:

something to celebrate / something to take pride in / something to enjoy

something good / something special / something comforting

a joy / a delight / a gratitude

a strength / a power / a magic / an accomplishment

something to notice / something to feel / something to rejoice in

A New Year's spread:

something to release / something to carry forward / theme card and main lesson for the year / how to approach and navigate challenges / personal strengths to utilize / advice and guidance

something to look forward to / something to stop pressuring yourself about / a way to treat yourself

Specialty Spreads for Insight and Ritual

Moon Phases

Spreads that use the phases of the moon can help with reflection, manifestation, shadow work, and with letting go/bringing in. These spreads are particularly effective if drawn and read during the moon phase.

Dark / Balsamic moon:

something to consider / something to observe / something to feel

New Moon:

an idea to explore / a longing to acknowledge / a new opportunity to evaluate

Waxing moon:

a desire that is clarifying / a path to follow / an ambition to pursue

Full moon:

a gift to receive / an accomplishment to recognize / a way to stay present

Waning moon:

an emotion to recognize / a need to honor / something to release

Eclipse:

something to explore / something to revisit or review / something to be open to change within

Zodiacal Seasons

Use these spreads when you're interested in utilizing, understanding, or more deeply exploring the energy of a particular astrological sign. These spreads can be useful during their zodiacal season, but you might also feel drawn to spreads that are associated with signs that feature prominently in your own natal chart. Remember, too, that there are established astrological correspondences for each of the major arcana archetypes, so these spreads pair nicely with archetype spreads and may be useful for additional reflection work around your birth card, card of the year, or favorite archetype.

Aries:

a fire in your soul / a longing in your heart / an ambition or desire that's got you raring to go

Taurus:

something that keeps your steps steady / something that gives you pleasure / something that protects your peace

Gemini:

a twinkle in your eye / a curiosity to indulge / a perception to investigate

Cancer:

something to share / something to hold back / something to enjoy

Leo:

a way that you shine / a magic that you carry / a joy to indulge

Virgo:

something to attend to / something to leave alone / something to do for yourself

Libra:

a value within you / a beauty around you / a belonging to cherish

Scorpio:

something to release / something to grieve / something to transform

Sagittarius:

a journey to take / a change to make / a truth to question

Capricorn:

something to begin / something to complete / something to play with

Aquarius:

an old path / a new perspective / a way to find freedom

Pisces:

something really big / something really true / something really lovely

Wheel of the Year

Many tarot spreads have been created for the Wheel of the Year in full, particularly around predictions or timings. These spreads were created with the intention of exploring the major themes of each specific sabbat or holiday and do not include predictive prompts. Use these spreads to tap into the energy of the season and to honor any needs, desires, or questions that you may be working through during this time of the year.

Imbolc:

an intention to focus / a dream to nurture / a desire to release / a cycle to renew / a blessing to celebrate

Ostara / Spring Equinox:

an inner light / an inner shadow / a way to balance light and dark / a rebirth to be aware of / an old pattern to release / a new seed to celebrate

Beltane:

a foundation for your fire / a blaze within you that burns brightly / an ember of energy to feed / a way that you share your flames with others / an inferno that needs some attention / a hidden spark that is waiting for you

Litha / Summer Solstice:

what is the source of your inner light and passion? / where do you shine the most brightly? / where could you use more fire? / how can you find your deepest potential this season? / what message should you carry forward this summer?

Lammas:

a fruit to reap with gratitude / a plant to keep tending / a seed to save for the future / a way to give back / a reminder to carry forward

Mabon / Autumn Equinox:

something to harvest and celebrate / something to release and honor / something to remember with gratitude / a place to show myself grace / a way to maintain balance in the coming months

Samhain:

an ending to honor / a way to grieve / a way to celebrate / a gift from your shadows / a rebirth to anticipate

Yule / Winter Solstice:

a secret wish / a necessary release / a lesson to accept / a fear to address / a gift to activate / a path forward

Archetypes

As with the zodiacal spreads shared earlier, these archetype spreads were written to help you explore each of the twenty-two major arcana archetypes. Each spread can help you focus on or more deeply understand the various energies of each card and can be particularly helpful when intentionally working with an archetype (or if an archetype shows up in a reading, and you aren't sure what it may indicate).

In Part Two of this book (see page 89), I talked about the need to clarify a reading when a meaning is unclear, or when a particular card is tripping you up. These spreads, in particular, can be helpful for addressing confusion with archetypes in readings. Allow me to offer a quick example of how you could use one of these spreads.

Let's say you wrote yourself a three-card spread, based on the suggestions in the section on Reflection and Self-Awareness (page 200). The prompts you choose are *something you love / something you need / something you are being offered.* You pull the following cards:

SOMETHING YOU LOVE

SOMETHING YOU NEED

SOMETHING OFFERED

Upon seeing the Empress in the second position, serving as an answer to the prompt something you need, you might find yourself floundering. Perhaps this doesn't make sense to you or doesn't quite resonate. After working through the first reading, you might decide that you want to do additional work with the Empress, to more deeply understand what this archetype might have to offer you as medicine right now. Using the prompts from the Empress archetype spread, you do another reading.

Each of these prompts offers some new perspectives on the Empress and can offer you various pathways to working with the Empress in more intimate, personal ways. And after doing this second reading, you can bring your discoveries and revelations on what the Empress might have to offer you back to your first, original reading, and perhaps uncover some new answers.

Fool:

a dream or idea that is taking shape / a fear or anxiety to recognize / a blessing or opportunity to embrace / something to be excited about

Magician:

your magic / how your magic manifests / what your magic craves / how to use your magic

Priestess:

something to observe / something to feel / something to hear

Empress:

an expression to let out / an abundance to share / a celebration to enjoy

Emperor:

something you're building / where you need structure / how to take control / resources to remember

Hierophant:

something you know / something you don't know / a question to ask / an answer to explore

Lovers:

a way that you are safe / a way that you are loved / a way that you are responsible

Chariot:

what you are learning / what requires more attention / what it all means

Strength:

how your patience feels / how your strength feels / something steady / something ready

Hermit:

your light / your shadow / something to surrender / a truth to spend more time with

Wheel:

where you are / where you're going / what's changing / what's staying the same

Justice:

something that is balanced / something that is off balance / a truth to see / a change to make

Hanged One:

stop struggling / take a deep breath and listen / surrender / change your perspective

Death:

an ending / a feeling / something you can rely on / something that may soon begin

Temperance:

something coming together / something splitting apart / a good friction

Devil:

pay attention / loosen up / be honest with yourself / take back your power

Tower:

something you are being called to release / a way to release it / something to remember if you feel afraid / a way to care for yourself through this shift

Star:

a shining light to follow / something to believe in / a next step

Moon:

something confusing / something clear / something strange / something magical

Sun:

a success to be proud of / a connection that is blossoming / a way you show up in the world / a beam of light to dance in

Judgement:

the old you / the current you / the next you / something to carry forward

World:

slow down / let yourself celebrate / relax

Elements

These two-card spreads are excellent for element studies, connecting to zodiacal seasons, or activating an element that you feel could be particularly supportive.

Fire: embers / ash

Air: fog / clarity

Water: shallows / depths

Earth: rooting / flowering

Metal: forming / dissolving

Wood: sprouting / solidifying

Spirit: seeing / feeling

Numerology

These two-card spreads can offer insights into what each digit can gift you as medicine. If you find yourself seeing the same number over and over in your life or your readings, these spreads can help you investigate broader themes that may be coming up.

0: beginning / ending

1: sparking / opening

2: choosing / seeing

3: expressing / creating

4: protecting / providing

5: challenging / exploring

6: stabilizing / enjoying

7: questioning / realizing

8: pursuing / empowering

9: offering / receiving

10: completing / renewing

11: imagining / delivering

22: establishing / empowering

33: envisioning / encompassing

CLOSING THOUGHTS

Working with tarot spreads, just like so many other aspects of a personal spiritual practice, is a wildly individual thing. It's my sincere hope that in exploring the different methods for reading, writing, and revising tarot spreads, you have a clearer picture of just how much you can do with these layouts. Remember that a tarot spread is just a blueprint, a layout, a starting place—it's your magic, your customizations, your interpretations, and your efforts that make the spread (and the tarot reading) come to life.

I know that the urge to do things perfectly the very first time is a strong one. But please hear me: Tarot spreads are infinitely changeable, and there's really no such thing as a perfect spread. There's simply the spread that is great for what you're doing right now, that captures your question, that gives you space to explore and investigate and discover. Cut yourself some slack, play around with everything, and see what happens.

The more you read tarot spreads, the easier it will become. The more you write original spreads, the clearer and more focused they'll get. And the more you revise existing spreads to suit your needs, the better you'll understand what you love to see in your spreads—and what you don't.

Happy reading!

RESOURCES FOR FURTHER EXPLORATION

78 Acts of Liberation by Lane Smith

The Cards You're Dealt by Theresa Reed

Cartomancy in Folk Witchcraft by Roger J. Horne

The Complete Book of Tarot Reversals by Mary K. Greer

The Four Elements of the Wise by Ivo Dominguez Jr.

The Psychic Art of Tarot by Mat Auryn

Queering the Tarot by Cassandra Snow

Radical Tarot by Charlie Claire Burgess

Red Tarot by Christopher Marmolejo

Secrets of Romani Fortune Telling by Jezmina Von Thiele and Paulina Stevens

Tarot for Change by Jessica Dore

Tarot for the Hard Work by Maria Minnis

The Tarot Handbook: Practical Applications of Ancient Visual Symbols by Angeles Arrien

The Tarot: History, Symbolism, and Divination by Robert M. Place

A Walk through the Forest of Souls by Rachel Pollack

The Witch's Book of Numbers by Rebecca Scolnick

ACKNOWLEDGMENTS

Books and works and projects like this are always part of bigger conversations, labors of love woven by many hands and minds. Sending endless gratitude and appreciation:

> To the tarot teachers and deck creators of past, present, and future; to everyone who has seen magic in these images and translated them into languages we can all speak. You are the reason we do what we do, that I do what I do. Keep making, keep writing, keep questioning, keep going.
>
> To my readers and clients, for your insatiable curiosity and your loving trust; for telling me what you need and letting me offer a few answers out of infinite possibilities.
>
> To the modern queer tarot readers who have helped me recontextualize the history of the cards, challenged my own notions of what these cards can represent, and courageously expanded far beyond the so-called standardized interpretations. I love that it feels like we are somehow remaking the tarot in our own image. Tarot is for all of us, and y'all are the ones that help me see that every day.
>
> To my agent Jill, for always saying *yes*. To my editor Kathryn, for always saying *yes and*. And to Eryn and the Weiser team, for showing me how beautiful and easy this process can be.

To my D&D group, for reminding me what structured imagination looks like and for helping me remember how to articulate what I already know. To my dear friends and community, who remind me that this work matters, even when I get lost in it.

To my beautiful, brilliant wife Jeanna, for being my partner in creative work and spiritual inspiration; for asking questions that I get to discover the answers to; for thinking I'm profound even when I don't know what's coming together; for demonstrating for me the bountiful potential in boundaries. Thank you for strengthening my Saturn (and for typing up these acknowledgments as I dictate them to you in a Spanish wine bar during our honeymoon).

And to you, clever Mercury, for beckoning me down such strange paths and giving me the words to describe what I find there. To you, sweet Spica, for your generosity and your grace, for supporting my light-filled devotions and rebellious dreams. Where shall we all go next?

ABOUT THE AUTHOR

Meg Jones Wall (she/they) is a queer, chronically ill tarot reader and teacher, who creates tarot resources and courses for spiritual misfits through her business, 3am.tarot. Meg is also the author of *Finding the Fool: A Tarot Journey to Radical Transformation,* with a third tarot book forthcoming. They are based in NYC.

TO OUR READERS

Weiser Books, an imprint of Red Wheel/Weiser, publishes books across the entire spectrum of occult, esoteric, speculative, and New Age subjects. Our mission is to publish quality books that will make a difference in people's lives without advocating any one particular path or field of study. We value the integrity, originality, and depth of knowledge of our authors.

Our readers are our most important resource, and we appreciate your input, suggestions, and ideas about what you would like to see published.

Visit our website at *www.redwheelweiser.com*, where you can learn about our upcoming books and free downloads, and also find links to sign up for our newsletter and exclusive offers.

You can also contact us at *info@rwwbooks.com* or at

Red Wheel/Weiser, LLC
65 Parker Street, Suite 7
Newburyport, MA 01950